INTRODUCING

POSTMODERNISM

RICHARD APPIGNANESI & CHRIS GARRATT

with ZIAUDDIN SARDAR & PATRICK CURRY

This edition published in the UK
in 2007 by Icon Books Ltd.,
The Old Dairy, Brook Road,
Thriplow, Cambridge SG8 7RG
email: info@iconbooks.co.uk
www.introducingbooks.com

Sold in the UK, Europe, South Africa
and Asia by Faber and Faber Ltd.,
3 Queen Square, London WC1N 3AU
or their agents

Distributed in the UK, Europe, South
Africa and Asia by TBS Ltd., TBS
Distribution Centre, Colchester Road,
Frating Green, Colchester CO7 7DW

This edition published in Australia
in 2007 by Allen & Unwin Pty. Ltd.,
PO Box 8500, 83 Alexander Street,
Crows Nest, NSW 2065

Previously published in the UK
and Australia in 1995 under the title
Postmodernism for Beginners and in
1999 as *Introducing Postmodernism*;
second edition first published in 2003

Reprinted 1995, 1996, 1997, 1998, 1999,
2000 (twice), 2001, 2002, 2006

This edition published in the USA
in 2007 by Totem Books
Inquiries to Icon Books Ltd.,
The Old Dairy, Brook Road,
Thriplow, Cambridge
SG8 7RG, UK

First published in the USA in 2005

Distributed to the trade in the USA by
National Book Network Inc.,
4501 Forbes Boulevard, Suite 200,
Lanham, Maryland 20706

Distributed in Canada by
Penguin Books Canada,
90 Eglinton Avenue East, Suite 700,
Toronto, Ontario M4P 2YE

ISBN 978-1840465-75-4

Originating editor: Richard Appignanesi

Printed by Gutenberg Press, Malta

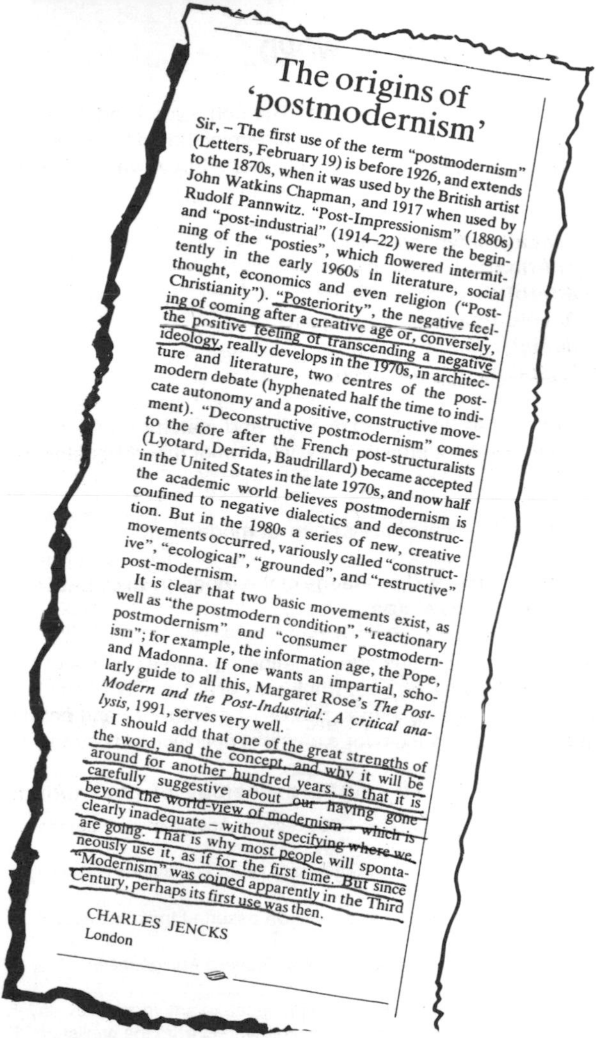

The origins of 'postmodernism'

Sir, – The first use of the term "postmodernism" (Letters, February 19) is before 1926, and extends to the 1870s, when it was used by the British artist John Watkins Chapman, and 1917 when used by Rudolf Pannwitz. "Post-Impressionism" (1880s) and "post-industrial" (1914–22) were the beginning of the "posties", which flowered intermittently in the early 1960s in literature, social thought, economics and even religion ("Post-Christianity"). "Posteriority", the negative feeling of coming after a creative age or, conversely, the positive feeling of transcending a negative ideology, really develops in the 1970s, in architecture and literature, two centres of the post-modern debate (hyphenated half the time to indicate autonomy and a positive, constructive movement). "Deconstructive postmodernism" comes to the fore after the French post-structuralists (Lyotard, Derrida, Baudrillard) became accepted in the United States in the late 1970s, and now half the academic world believes postmodernism is confined to negative dialectics and deconstruction. But in the 1980s a series of new, creative movements occurred, variously called "constructive", "ecological", "grounded", and "restructive" post-modernism.

It is clear that two basic movements exist, as well as "the postmodern condition", "reactionary postmodernism" and "consumer postmodernism"; for example, the information age, the Pope, and Madonna. If one wants an impartial, scholarly guide to all this, Margaret Rose's *The Post-Modern and the Post-Industrial: A critical analysis*, 1991, serves very well.

I should add that one of the great strengths of the word, and the concept, and why it will be around for another hundred years, is that it is carefully suggestive about our having gone beyond the world-view of modernism – which is clearly inadequate – without specifying where we are going. That is why most people will spontaneously use it, as if for the first time. But since "Modernism" was coined apparently in the Third Century, perhaps its first use was then.

CHARLES JENCKS
London

Charles Jencks, an authority on postmodern architecture and art, provides a useful scanning of the term **postmodern**. But what does it mean in practice? Does "postmodern" accurately sum up the story of what we are living at present? Or is it just a fashionable term that leaves us unenlightened about our true historical condition?

First, let's consider the WORD...

What do you mean **post**modern? The confusion is advertised by the "post" prefixed to "modern". Postmodernism identifies itself by something it isn't. It isn't modern anymore. But in what sense exactly is it **post**...

- as a **result** of modernism?
-the **aftermath** of modernism?
-the **afterbirth** of modernism?
-the **development** of modernism?
-the **denial** of modernism?
-the **rejection** of modernism?

Postmodern has been used in a mix-and-match of some or all of these meanings. Postmodernism is a confusion of meanings stemming from two riddles...

-it resists and obscures the **sense** of modernism

-it implies a complete knowledge of the modern which has been surpassed by a **new age**.

A new age? An age, any age, is defined by the evidence of historic changes in the way we **see, think** and **produce.** We can identify these changes as belonging to the spheres of **art, theory** and **economic history**, and explore them for a practical definition of postmodernism.

Let's begin with art by tracing the **genealogy of postmodern art**.

PART ONE: THE GENEALOGY OF POSTMODERN ART

We could begin by visiting an installation by the Conceptual artist Daniel Buren (b.1939), entitled **On two levels with two colours** (1976), which features a vertically striped band at the floor levels of two adjoining gallery rooms, one at a step up from the other. Empty rooms, nothing else...

Buren's installation is not necessarily a representative example of art in the postmodern age. But it is a good place to start from, in the sense of where modernism itself has **arrived at** through a persistent history of innovation.

What's Modern? The Shock of the Old

Modern comes from the Latin word **modo**, meaning "just now". Since when have we been modern? For a surprisingly long time, as the following example shows.

Around 1127, the Abbot Suger began reconstructing his abbey basilica of St. Denis in Paris. His architectural ideas resulted in something never seen before, a "new look" neither classically Greek nor Roman nor Romanesque.
Suger didn't know what to call it, so he fell back on the Latin, **opus modernum. A modern work.**

Suger helped to inaugurate an immensely influential architectural style which became known as the **Gothic.**

Gothic was in fact a term of abuse, coined by Italian Renaissance theorists, meaning a northern or German **barbaric style.** The ideal style of Renaissance architects and artists was the classical Greek, or what they called the **antica e buona maniera moderna** - the ancient and good modern style.

Ever since then, architects have been arguing about what best represents a perennial style - classical, gothic, modern or even postmodern.

Dialectical Antagonism

At least since medieval times, there has been a motivating sense of antagonism between "then" and "now", between ancient and modern. Historical periods in the West have followed one another in **disaffinity** with what has gone before. A rejection of one's immediate predecessors seems almost instinctively generational.

The result of this historical **dialectic** (from the Greek, **debate** or **discourse**) is that Western culture recognizes no single tradition.

History is carved up into conceptual periods -

Medieval

Renaissance

Baroque

Romantic

and so on. These antagonistic periods are Western culture's **sets** of tradition, a sort of "periodic table" of tradition.

Tradition in the West is constituted and indeed **energized** by what is in combat with it.

Another peculiarity of Western culture is its strongly **historicist bias**, a belief that history determines the way things are and **must be**.

WHAT WE PRODUCE IS ALWAYS MILES AHEAD OF WHAT WE THINK.
Darling, it's arrived... WORKLESS WASHDAYS at last!

Karl Marx's **dialectical materialism** provided the classic historicist formula.

Marxism established a structural difference between society's traditional or cultural institutions and its economic productive forces. Rapid-paced progress occurs in the **infrastructure**, the economic sphere of productive activities which supports but also subverts the **superstructure**, the social sphere of ideology which includes religion, art, politics, law and all **traditional attitudes**. The superstructure evolves more slowly and is more resistant to change than the economic infrastructure, especially in the modern industrial age of advanced capitalism.

Ideas always chase the material world. From their origin they are out of date. Nietzsche — words are dead ideas.

The ways we think - or better, those assumptions we take for granted - are pre-established by superstructural **ideologies**.

"Mankind always takes up only such problems as it can solve...we will always find that the problem itself arises only when the material conditions for its solution already exist or are at least in the process of formation."

Karl Marx, preface to **A Contribution to the Critique of Political Economy** (1859)

What's MODERNISM?

The Marxian formula is still useful for understanding the different **speed-lanes of change** in the traditional and productive spheres of society.

Modernism, in the infrastructural productive sense, begins in the 1890s and 1900s, a time which experienced mass technological innovations, the second tidal wave of the Industrial Revolution begun nearly a century before.

New Technology

•the internal combustion and diesel engines; steam turbine electricity generators
•electricity and petrol as new sources of power
•the automobile, bus, tractor and aeroplane
•telephone, typewriter and tape machine as the basics of modern office and systems management
•chemical industry's production of synthetic materials - dyes, man-made fibres and plastics
•new engineering materials - reinforced concrete, aluminium and chromium alloys

Mass Media and Entertainment

•advertising and mass circulation newspapers (1890s)
•the gramophone (1877); the Lumière brothers invent cinematography and Marconi the wireless telegraph (1895)
•Marconi's first radio wave transmission (1901)
•first movie theatre, the Pittsburgh Nickelodeon (1905)

Science

•genetics established in the 1900s
•Freud launches psychoanalysis (c.1900)
•discovery of uranium and radium radioactivity by Becquerel and the Curies (1897-9)
•Rutherford's revolutionary new model of the atom overturns classical physics (1911)
•Max Planck's quantum theory of energy (1900) revised by Niels Bohr and Rutherford (1913)
•Einstein's Special and General theories of Relativity (1905 and 1916)

It isn't difficult to see how these innovations extend logically to postmodern scientific and information developments. Two examples...

1. The foundations of postmodern cosmology - atomic theory, quantum and Relativity - were laid down between the 1890s and 1916.

2. The modern copper telephone wire replaced with the postmodern fibre-optic cable increases the information data-load 250,000 times over (the entire contents of Oxford's Bodleian Library transmitted in 42 seconds).

Modernism in the cultural or superstructural sense occupies the same period in the early 1900s - the heroic first phase of modernist experimentation in literature, music, the visual arts and architecture.

Picasso's Big Bang

Despite the telephone, telegraphy and other such technological novelties, a photographic glimpse of everyday life **circa** 1907 looks to us entirely remote from "modernity". Nothing prepares us - or indeed the good folk of 1907 - for the first truly modernist painting, Picasso's **Les Demoiselles d'Avignon**, 1907.

Those angular deformities and staring African mask faces depict prostitutes, partly expressing Picasso's own panic about syphilis but, more importantly, proclaiming a new **anti-representational** model of [de]FORM[ation].

WHY HAS THIS VIOLENCE TO REALISTIC REPRESENT-
-ATION IN ART COME ABOUT?

The Crisis of Representation

Some art historians have argued, to an extent correctly, that the invention of photography ended the authority of painting to reproduce reality. Painting pictures of "reality" had simply become obsolete. Technological innovation in the infrastructure had outstripped the superstructural traditions of visual art. Mass production (photography) replaced hand-crafted originality (art).

YES! THAT'S GREAT!... SAY CHEESE.. NOW...HOLD IT FOR 3MINS 45SECS...
H FOX TALBOT
THE NUMBER ONE
NAME IN PHOTOGRAPH
PRINTS READY BY 4-30

The crisis runs deeper than this crude but effective scenario suggests. The doctrine of **realism** itself was coming to an end. Realism depends on a **mirror theory** of knowledge, essentially that the mind is a mirror of reality. Objects existing outside the mind can be **represented** (reproduced by a concept or work of art) in a way that is adequate, accurate and true.

Cézanne: the View Contains the Viewer

Paul Cézanne (1839-1906) did not scrap realism but revised it to include **uncertainty** in our perception of things. Representation had to account for the effect of **interaction** between seeing and the object, the variations of viewpoint and possibilities of doubt in what one sees.

Cézanne had taken a revolutionary new direction, painting not **reality** but the effect of **perceiving** it.

Cézanne was not interested simply to reproduce a fragmented, subjective view of reality. He sought after a basic foundation, a "unified field" theory that must underlie the variability of perception, and this he got from elementary **geometric solids**. In a famous letter of 1904, he advised, "...treat nature by the cylinder, the sphere, the cone."

The "Science" of Cubism

C
D
A
B
THE UNCERTAINTY PRINCIPLE WAS NOT MINE: IT WAS THE DISCOVERY OF PHYSICIST WERNER HEISENBERG (1901–76), FORMULATED IN 1927 AS A CONSEQUENCE OF QUANTUM MECHANICS. IN SIMPLEST TERMS, IT STATES THAT THERE IS ALWAYS UNCERTAINTY IN SIMULTANEOUS MEAS--UREMENTS OF THE POSITION OF A PARTICLE...
OUR ALBERT
..... AND THE UNIFIED FIELD THEORY WAS MY LIFETIME QUEST TO DEMONSTRATE HOW ALL NATURE'S FORCES DERIVE FROM ONE COMMON UNITY AND A SINGLE ULTIMATE LAW OF ACTION!
HOW CAN YOU BE SO SURE?

Cézanne was not a physicist, modern or otherwise. Nor indeed were his successors and heirs, the Cubists. What we have is one of those rare occasions in history when science and art arrive independently at complementary attitudes.

Cubism, unleashed by Picasso's **Demoiselles d'Avignon**, was then developed by him, Georges Braque and others between 1907 and 1914.
A typical Cubist painting, Picasso's **Girl with a Mandolin** (1910), takes Cézanne's theories of **variability** and **stability** to an astounding logical conclusion.

The human figure simplified to geometry, interacting on a par with the space around it and treated like architecture, might be said to be **dehumanized**. Cubism agreed with modern physics in rejecting the notion of a single isolatable event - the view contains the viewer. This is not necessarily a dehumanizing limit but a recognition that the human is **non-exceptional** to reality.

The End of Original Art?

"Reproducible reality" was left to photography, while art took a quantum leap in a new Cubist direction. Cubism rescued art from obsolescence and re-established its authority to represent reality in a way that photography could not.

But photography threatened both traditional and avantgarde art in another sense not recognized until later, in 1936, when the Marxist critic Walter Benjamin published his essay, **The Work of Art in the Age of Mechanical Reproduction**.

I SAW THAT THE AUTHORITY OR AUTONOMY OF ORIGINAL WORKS OF ART DERIVES FROM THEIR ***UNREPRODUCIBILITY*** — (EXCEPT AS FAKES) - WHICH GIVES THEM A MAGICAL **AURA**, A CHARISMATIC HALO THAT SURROUNDS AUTHENTIC ART OBJECTS BECAUSE THEY ARE "ONE-OFFS", UNIQUE, IRREPLACEABLE AND HENCE PRICELESS.

He argued that this aura - this fetish of sacred uniqueness - would now be eliminated by **mass reproduction**, essentially by the photographic printing of original works of art in widely distributed books, posters, postcards and even postage stamps.

The mechanical reproducibility of original art must inevitably have a disintegrating effect on "originality" itself.

But for the viewer a new idea is always new. An original experience.

Modern is Postmodern

The modern is always historically at war with what comes immediately before it. In this same sense, modern is always post-**something**.

The modern ends up being at war with itself and must inevitably become **post**-modern.

This weird logic of becoming postmodern is signalled by the Latin origin of modern, **modo**, "just now". Postmodern therefore literally means "after just now".

Curiously, a useful definition of postmodern art arises from this dilemma of "just now" negating the preceding "just now". According to the French philosopher Jean-François Lyotard...

What, then, is the postmodern?... It is undoubtedly a part of the modern. All that has been received, if only yesterday...must be suspected. What space does Cézanne challenge? The Impressionists'. What object do Picasso and Braque attack? Cézanne's. What presupposition does Duchamp break with in 1912? That which says one must make a painting, be it Cubist. And (Daniel) Buren questions that other presupposition which he believes had survived untouched in the work of Duchamp: the place of presentation of the work. In an amazing acceleration, the generations precipitate themselves. A work can become modern only if it is first postmodern. Postmodernism thus understood is not modernism at its end but in the nascent state, and this state is constant.

The Postmodern Condition (1979)

Well, in fact, it might not be. Let's continue tracing our genealogy to see how or if or at what break-off point we arrive at postmodern art.

The Sublime

Lyotard also provides an equally useful definition of **modern** art. Modern art for him is that which presents " the fact that the unpresentable exists. To make visible that there is something which can be conceived and which can neither be seen nor made visible: this is what is at stake in modern painting."

WHAT WE CAN CONCEIVE OF – THE INFINITELY GREAT, FOR INSTANCE – BUT IS NOT IN OUR POWER TO ***REPRESENT***, EXACTLY DEFINES THE ***SUBLIME***.

The only way to present what is conceivable but not representable is **abstraction**.

Lyotard rightly mentions the Russian artist Kasimir Malevich (1878-1935) who in 1915 "presented the unrepresentable Sublime" by painting a white square on a white background.
Malevich's own 1919 **Manifesto of Suprematism** makes plain that he knew he was representing the sublime.

Genealogy of a Modernist tree

The paintings of Piet Mondrian (1872-1944) show clearly the radical modernist evolution of a tree

from **representation** to minimal pure **abstraction.**

ABSTRACTION ALONE IS NOT ENOUGH TO ELIMINATE THE NATURALISTIC FROM PAINTING. LINE AND COLOUR MUST BE COMPOSED OTHERWISE THAN IN NATURE.
ELLOW
RED
BLU

Mondrian's abstract art attempted to purge itself of all representational references - to banish any "illustration" of reality.

Clive Bell, a British art critic, put the extremist case for a pure modernist aesthetic in 1914.

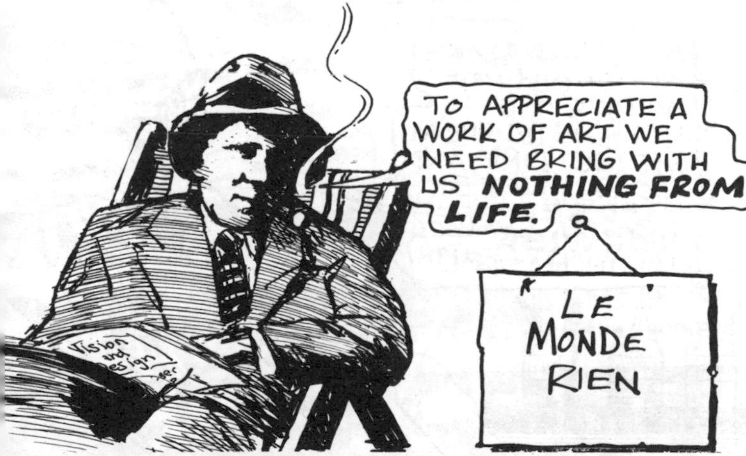

Malevich, Mondrian and other pioneering abstractionists were self-consciously solving the "crisis of representation". The **concept** - inadequate to represent reality - is rescued by elevating it and eliminating all traces of "reality" from the (re)presentation of the unpresentable. The concept itself becomes Sublime Reality (one is tempted to say, **hyper**-reality, but this is postmodern lingo).

Machine-Aesthetic Optimism

Mondrian, a member of the Dutch **De Stijl** group, shared an ambition with many other artists from different but parallel schools - **Cubism,** the Weimar **Bauhaus**, Italian **Futurism**, Russian **Constructivism** and other varieties.

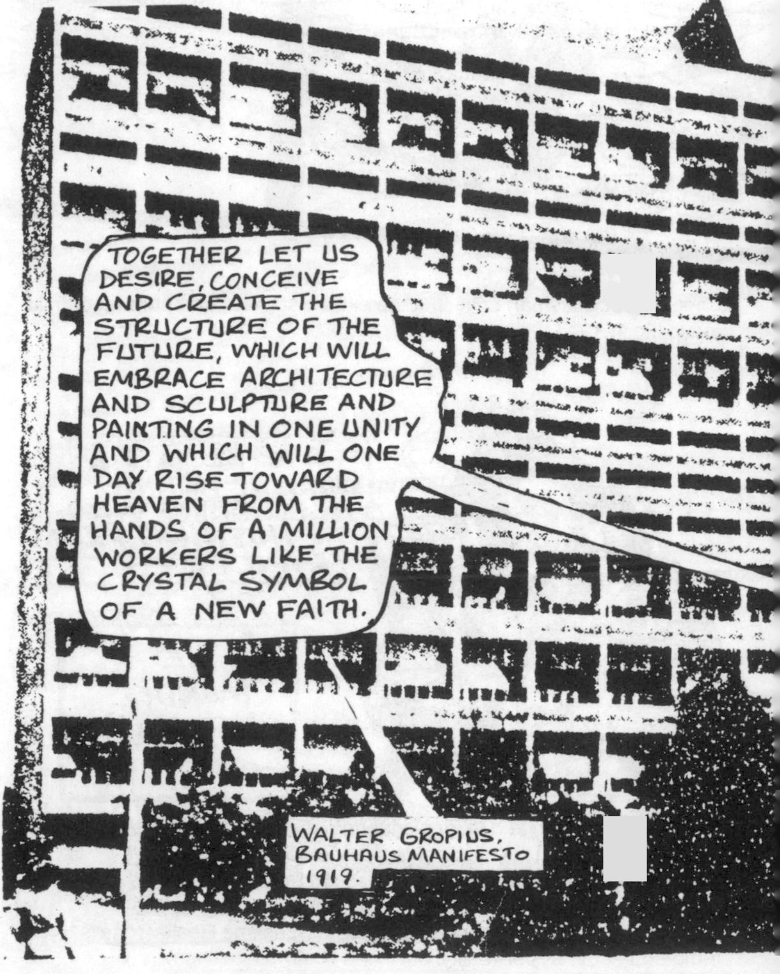
TOGETHER LET US DESIRE, CONCEIVE AND CREATE THE STRUCTURE OF THE FUTURE, WHICH WILL EMBRACE ARCHITECTURE AND SCULPTURE AND PAINTING IN ONE UNITY AND WHICH WILL ONE DAY RISE TOWARD HEAVEN FROM THE HANDS OF A MILLION WORKERS LIKE THE CRYSTAL SYMBOL OF A NEW FAITH.
WALTER GROPIUS, BAUHAUS MANIFESTO 1919.

They all embraced what is loosely called a **machine aesthetic**, an optimistic belief in the role of abstraction in human life and an emphasis on machine-like, undecorated flat surfaces. Their aim was to form a universally applicable "modern style", **reproducible** anywhere, trancending all national cultures.
The modern architecture we are most familiar with (and which is most condemned nowadays by postmodernists) grew out of these trends and was rightly named the **International style**. Its most notorious practitioners were Mies van der Rohe, Walter Gropius and Le Corbusier ("buildings - machines designed for living in").

RIGHT ON, WALT!
LIFT NOT WORKING PLEASE USE STAIRS

Constructivism

Cubism in Russia advanced towards **Constructivism** (1914-20), the abandonment of easel painting in favour of kinetic art and technical design applied to typography, architecture and industrial production.

Constructivism, as its propagandist name suggests, was an eager "constructive" supporter of the 1917 Bolshevik revolution.

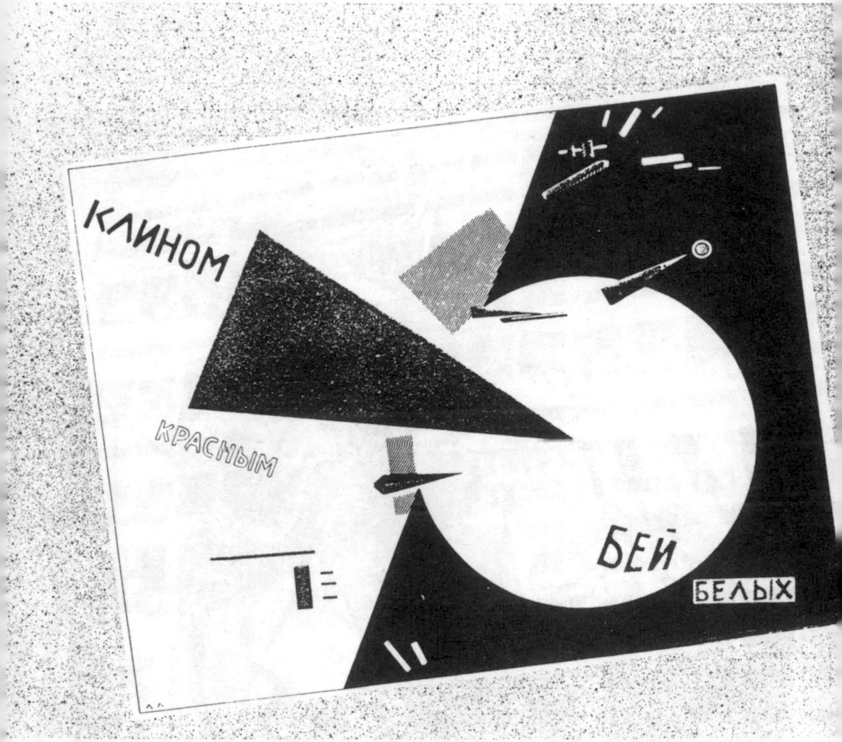

This optimistically utopian art co-existed at first happily and very productively with the Leninist phase of the revolution (1918-24). Thereafter it began to run into conflict with the official, orthodox Communist party-line on art.

Stalinist Totalitarianism

In the 1930s' era of Stalinism, Constructivism was suppressed as un-Marxist "formalism". The official party-line adopted a propaganda style of heroic realism, named **socialist realism.**

Utopian modernism which had aimed at being internationally reproducible was rejected in favour of a realism "comprehensible" to the masses and a reproducible model for other countries aspiring to Communism.

Also in the 1930s, totalitarian Nazi Germany prohibited modern art as decadent, non-Aryan and sub-human. A mix of saccharine soft porn and heroic realism became the dogma.

The Tragic Failure of Abstract Expressionism

Totalitarian art, Stalinist or Nazi, with its re-institution of realism, had two post-war effects. It confirmed modernist abstraction as the alternative style of the democratic free world and put the last nail in realism's coffin.

Hardly surprisingly, America turned to its own domestic breed of emerging abstract art for this confirmation, which it christened **Abstract Expressionism** in 1946 (a term first coined in 1919 to describe the Russian Wassily Kandinsky's abstract paintings).

Jackson Pollock (1912-56) stands as the archetypal hero and tragic victim of Abstract Expressionism. Pollock and other Abstract Expressionists viewed their art as emotionally super-charged with meaning.
Pollock also confessed the sources for his "all-over drip" action paintings...

Much to the consternation of Pollock and his colleagues, Abstract Expressionism was hijacked by the American art establishment and promoted internationally as 100% pure American, purely **formal** abstract art. It now seems almost a knee-jerk reaction: if official Communism banned "formalism", then formalism must be an essential constituent of free enterprise democracy.
Cold War strategy demanded a "true American" identity, distinct from Europe and the epidemic of Communism, particularly in the early 1950s and Senator McCarthy's anti-Communist witch-hunts.

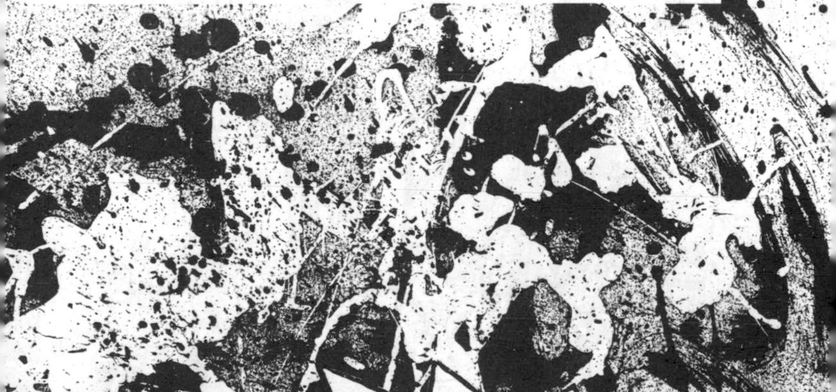

Pollock and a remarkable number of his school fell victims to alcoholism, premature death and suicide. Abstract Expressionism was the last act of romantic modernism played out on hostile American terrain.

DADA!

Surrealism, one of Pollock's sources, was the successor movement to **Dadaism** (1916-24). Dadaism upsets the notion that early modernist art was entirely optimistic. Born screaming out of the mouths of Hugo Ball, Tristan Tzara and others at the Cabaret Voltaire in Zurich, 1916, it raged briefly as an international wildfire. It was, and with surprising durability, remains vitally influential.

Dadaism arose in nihilist protest to the vast mechanized assembly-line slaughter of World War One - the last war ever to be fought between imperial dynasties (British, German, Austrian, Russian, Italian, Japanese etc.) and the first to exploit modern technology - machine-guns, poison gas, tanks and airplanes.

Dadaism was a temporary meeting-point for some of modernism's pioneering artists - Hans Arp, Max Ernst, Francis Picabia and Marcel Duchamp. **Kurt Schwitters** (1887-1948) was a singularly fertile Dadaist in Hanover, Germany, notorious for his **Merz** productions (**merz** suggests the French **merde**, shit). His **Merz** pictures and **Merzbaus** (environmental assemblies of rubbish), **Merz** concrete poems and performances, new alphabet and so on, are at the origin of practically every manifestation of later "post"-modern art.

EVERYTHING THE ARTIST SPITS IS ART!
Kurt Schwitters.

Dadaism was crucially important for releasing - or unleashing - **automatism**, a junking of all traditional rules of art in favour of **chance** as the direct creative access to the unconscious. Pollock's "drip" action paintings closely answer to the prescription of automatism later theorized by Surrealism.

Marcel Duchamp and the Readymades

The optimistic innovators of Cubism, confronted by the mechanized barbarism of WW1, had to reconsider themselves. **Marcel Duchamp** (1887-1968) foresightedly predated this crisis in 1912 when he painted his last Cubist canvas, **Nude descending a staircase**, and began thinking along Dada lines before the name existed.

By 1912, direct incorporations of non-artistic readymade materials in the painting - bits of newspaper, textiles, chair wickerwork, tin - had become part of the Cubist vocabulary developed by Picasso, Braque and others.

Duchamp was the first to realize that any "readymade" non-art object **on its own** could be displayed as "art" if dissociated from its original context, use and meaning. His best-known examples of readymade art are a **Bottlerack** (1914) and a porcelain **Urinal** signed R. Mutt (1917).

?
VIN
IF IT'S SIGNED AND YOU CAN'T PISS IN IT BECAUSE IT'S STUCK ON A MUSEUM WALL -IT'S GOT TO BE ART, — WHAT ELSE?

The mass-(re)produced object displaced the very idea of artistic originality and the sacred uniqueness of the original work of art. Duchamp opened a can of worms. His readymades had unforeseen consequences that have culminated in the dilemmas of postmodern art. Let's see what these predicaments are - which in each case have been posed as **answers**...

The Aura of the Artist

The aura and autonomy of the original work of art can end up transferred to the artist's own charisma value. The artist "as such" becomes the auratic art object, as in the blatant case of the London artists Gilbert and George who displayed themselves as "living sculptures" in 1970.

Here too Duchamp had led the way by focusing publicity on himself as the enigma who "renounced" art to play chess instead. The artist as pretended Sphinx is also a readymade ploy.

The Event

Another closely allied neo-Dadaist tactic is the transference of aura to the event or happening, such as the classic happenings staged by American Pop artists Jim Dine and Claes Oldenburg in the early 1960s. **Yves Klein** (1928-62), a leading European neo-Dadaist, directed two naked women smeared with blue paint to roll about a canvas on the floor while a single-note "symphony" played in the background.

Installations

Josef Beuys (1921-86) combined a shamanistic aura (the artist as magician) with the fabrication of **installations** or environmental pieces.

Duchamp's installation of the readymade had the effect of radically upgrading the **power of display**. Installation shifts the empowerment of aura from the object to the **place**, in other words, the gallery or museum.

The Supreme Master of Po Mo Art?

And so we arrive at the most famous wig in art history, **Andy Warhol**['s] (1930-87), the Pope of Pop Art. Warhol turned mechanical reproduction itself into art by transferring a photo image to a silkscreen which is laid on the canvas and inked from the back. The only slight "human" touch in this Andycraft is an overlay of crudely applied synthetic colour.

Banal replications of Campbell's soup cans vie with images of deep-down morbidity - Marilyn Monroe after her suicide, Mrs Kennedy after JFK's assassination, mug shots of hoodlums, car accidents, the electric chair, gangster funerals and race riots.
Under Warhol's treatment, aesthetics turns into anaesthetics.

Hard to tell with Andy whether he's super-cool, prodigiously voyeuristic or just simply brain dead.
Warhol's look perfectly sums up the cliché slogan of postmodern wisdom: "What you see is what you get."
And the look goes back to the looker, Andy himself, narcissistic, aristocratic, implacably poker-faced **boredom**.

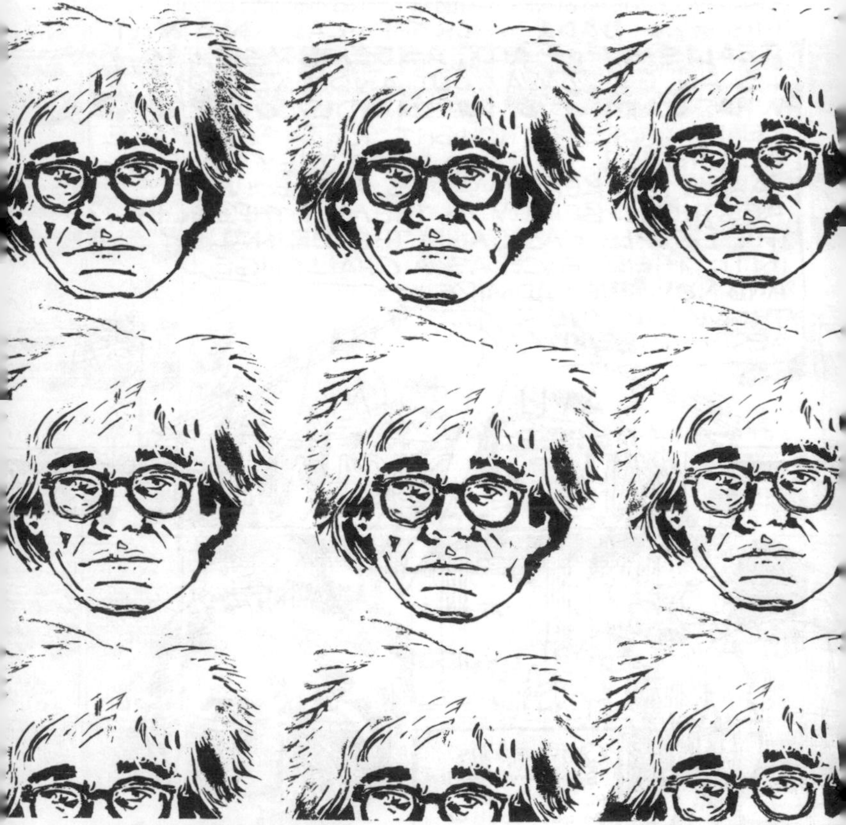

Warhol's reproductions are not about producing art or even the artist, but the Ultimate Commodity, **A Celebrity**. Aura is reduced to the Midas golden-touch word, FAMOUS, which transforms everything without changing anything.

Was Duchamp to Blame?

Is it unfair to make Duchamp responsible for opening the road to the postmodern predicament? Duchamp himself in 1962 protested against a discipleship that he bitterly rejected.

ENDGAME

Duchamp's complaint is deeply ironical. He is saying that his tactical brand of reproducibility - the readymades - was unique, one-off and **not reproducible.**

We've attempted to trace the "past" modern genealogy of postmodernism - but have we really arrived at "present" postmodernism?
For instance, is **Minimalism** postmodern? Carl André's **120 Fire-Bricks** (1968) at the Tate Gallery offered a notorious example.

Minimal art eliminated all elements of **expressiveness** - which left only the aesthetic process itself (or what was left of it) on the shrinking borderline of non-art.
Minimalism isn't properly postmodern because it is still absorbed in modernist experimentation initiated by forerunners like Kasimir Malevich.

Conceptual art (also in the 1960s) went further and threw out the aesthetic process altogether. "Art" itself was refuted as contaminated by the élitism and crass marketeering of the art world.

Piero Manzoni (1933-63) typified the movement (literally) when he canned his own shit and sold it, labelled **100% Pure Artist's Shit**.

Conceptualism still manifests itself in the 1990s with "anti-art" scandals, such as Damien Hirst's exhibit of a dead sheep in an aquarium of formaldehyde (1994), or sculptures in the artists' own blood or in urine...

Is this postmodern? Not really. Conceptualism's use of eccentric materials - Beuys' sculpture in fat, Richard Long's earthworks, or car wrecks or dead sheep - had been foreseen by Kurt Schwitters' **Merz** rubbish sculptures.

So, where are we?

We're keeping pace with modernity...

From the early 1900s to the 1970s, art underwent rapid modernizing changes without precedent in Western history. There have been three fundamental stages in modernism's progress.

from (1) crisis in the **representation** of reality ----------------------------------	Cézanne Cubism Dadaism Surrealism
to (2) the **presentation of the unpresentable** (abstraction)----------------------------------	Suprematism, De Stijl etc. Constructivism Abstract Expressionism Minimalism
and finally (3) **non-presentation** (abandoning the aesthetic process)----------------------------------	Conceptualism

Each new variation in modern art succeeded the one before in a consecutive series of **posts**-modernism: like spokes in a rotating flywheel that seem to blend together at high speed and vanish.

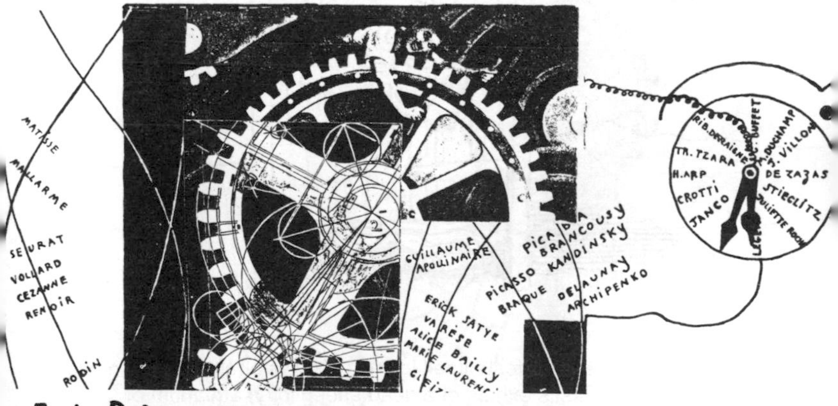

Expiry Date

In terms of the Marxian formula, it would seem that the superstructural traditions of art have shed themselves in the effort to innovate at a pace in rhythm with modernity's infrastructural advances in technology. To put it simply, art vanished in the high-velocity quest for originality. Such a quest was inevitably and fatally terminal.

Art can only progress towards its own self-annihilation.

False Postmodernisms

Does postmodern art finally mean **no art** - unless it is a **post-mortem** art resuscitated by two false brands of postmodernism?

WHAT DO YOU MEAN, FALSE POSTMODERNISM?

J.-F. Lyotard has unravelled and identified one alternative strand of postmodernism which is **anti-modernist**. It has been heard since the 1980s calling loudly for an **end to experimentation**, which receives wide populist media coverage. Anti-modernist conservatism is very much part of the so-called postmodern "outlook", a snarled cat's-cradle of dissenting views, which is one reason why rational consensus on postmodernism is impossible.

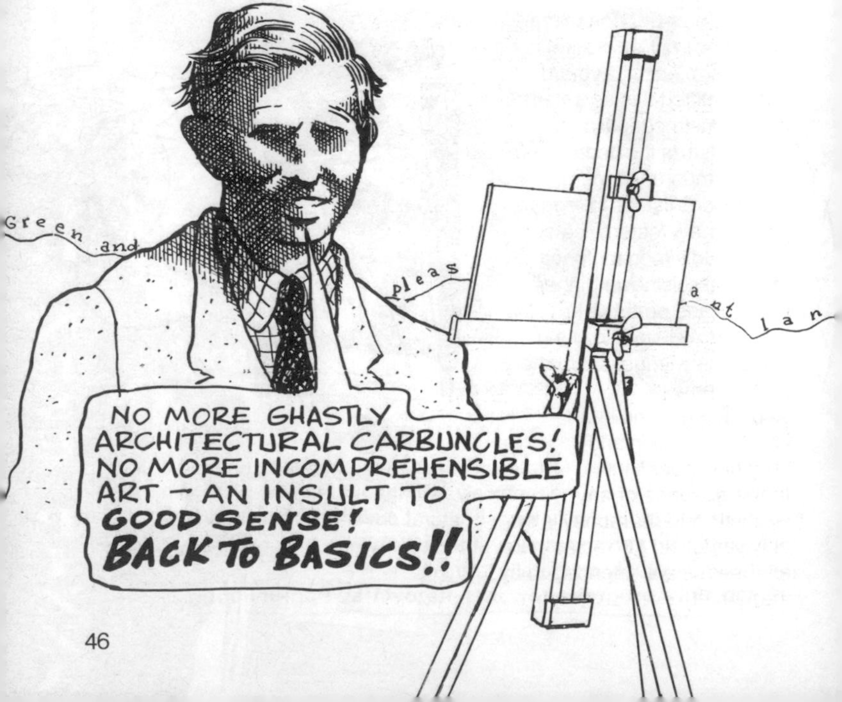
Green and
pleas
a nt lan
NO MORE GHASTLY ARCHITECTURAL CARBUNCLES! NO MORE INCOMPREHENSIBLE ART — AN INSULT TO GOOD SENSE! BACK TO BASICS!!

Eclectic Postmodernism

There is another bogus postmodernism which is perfectly adapted to the contemporary mono-cultural prevalence of free market capitalism. Again, Lyotard has identified this as **eclectic** or junk postmodernism.

Eclecticism is the degree zero of contemporary general culture: one listens to reggae, watches a Western, eats McDonald's food for lunch and local cuisine for dinner, wears Paris perfume in Tokyo and "retro" clothes in Hong Kong; knowledge is a matter for TV games.

And it's the same in art - kitsch, confusion and "anything goes".

In the absence of any æsthetic criteria, money is the only yardstick. All "tastes", like all "needs", are attended to by the market.

A "Real" Postmodernism?

If there is a "real" postmodernism, it is recognizable by three urgent items on its agenda.

The first item is the dilemma of **reproducibility** in the age of mass consumerism. Walter Benjamin's 1936 prophecy of an elimination of the aura and autonomy of original works of art through mass reproduction has not come true. We have seen it have the opposite effect. Multi-million dollar prices for originals might be said to be proportional to their availability in mass reproduction which has made them all the more desirable to own.

A **consumerist aura** now extends to anything with a halo of the relic - Marilyn Monroe's panties or Al Capone's Pontiac - or anything with nostalgia value - art deco radios, bracket phones, biscuit tins - because they are the souvenirs of yesteryear's ancient manufacture.

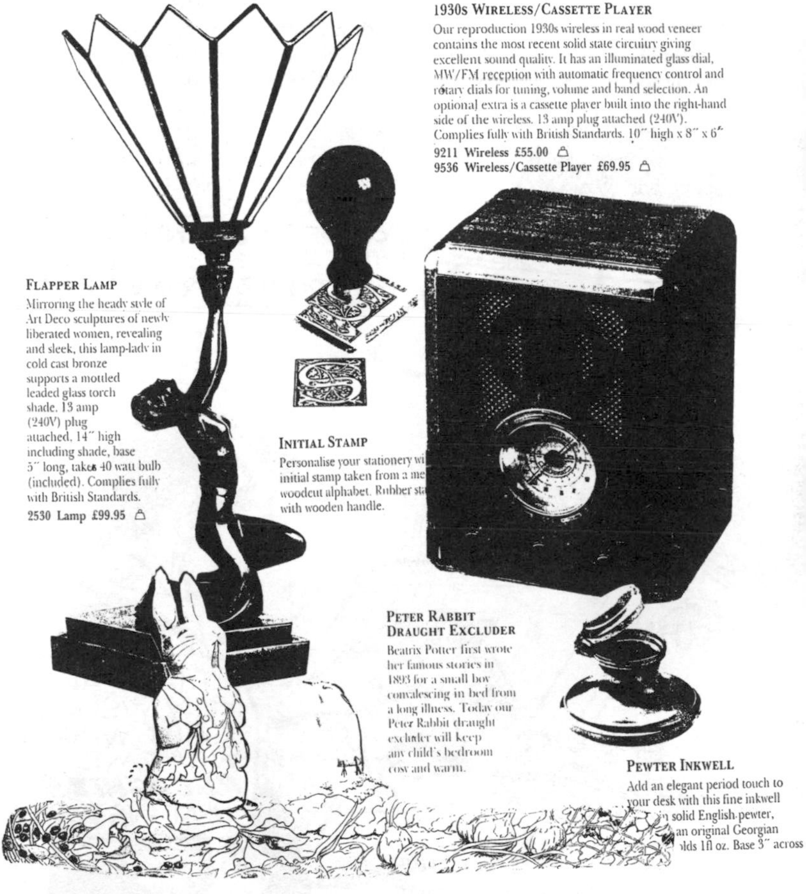
1930s Wireless/Cassette Player
Our reproduction 1930s wireless in real wood veneer contains the most recent solid state circuitry giving excellent sound quality. It has an illuminated glass dial, MW/FM reception with automatic frequency control and rotary dials for tuning, volume and band selection. An optional extra is a cassette player built into the right-hand side of the wireless. 13 amp plug attached (240V). Complies fully with British Standards. 10" high x 8" x 6"
9211 Wireless £55.00
9536 Wireless/Cassette Player £69.95
Flapper Lamp
Mirroring the heady style of Art Deco sculptures of newly liberated women, revealing and sleek, this lamp-lady in cold cast bronze supports a mottled leaded glass torch shade. 13 amp (240V) plug attached. 14" high including shade, base 5" long, takes 40 watt bulb (included). Complies fully with British Standards.
2530 Lamp £99.95
Initial Stamp
Personalise your stationery wi
initial stamp taken from a me
woodcut alphabet. Rubber sta
with wooden handle.
Peter Rabbit Draught Excluder
Beatrix Potter first wrote her famous stories in 1893 for a small boy convalescing in bed from a long illness. Today our Peter Rabbit draught excluder will keep any child's bedroom cosy and warm.
Pewter Inkwell
Add an elegant period touch to your desk with this fine inkwell
in solid English pewter,
an original Georgian
olds 1fl oz. Base 3" across

This is **image consumerism**. The reproduced is taking the place of reality or **replacing it as hyper-reality.**
We are living what has **already** been lived and **reproduced** with no reality anymore but that of the cannibalized image.

What you see is what you get...

How does the artist - or any concerned citizen of postmodernity - face the threat of unreal simulated hyperreality? You could accept it, of course ("anything goes"). Or you could carry on with experimentation, as Lyotard urges. But the trouble is, there are no longer any rules or categories by which to judge the experimentally unfamiliar. "Those rules and categories are what the work of art itself is looking for."

POSTMODERNISM MEANS WORKING WITHOUT RULES IN ORDER TO FIND OUT THE RULES OF WHAT YOU'VE DONE.
THAT'S ALL VERY WELL... ...BUT WHO OR WHAT WILL RECOGNIZE WHAT I'VE DONE?

The question isn't simply one of further experimentation, but of whose **power** will "legitimate" what is done as the right way of doing it. This brings us to the third and central issue of "real" postmodern concern. **Legitimation**.

Legitimation

A question we have so far delayed asking is: how did a difficult and unpopular avantgarde modern art become accepted as the institutional standard of taste? **Whose** taste is that? The taste of art galleries, museums, dealers and their art-buying public. In short, the merchants of art and its collectors.

Not even the most extreme challenges of anti-art have succeeded to undermine the art-dealing system. "Big-time commercial art-dealing is a classic example of a free market economy, now hard to discover elsewhere in so pure a form. The surprising thing is how successfully it has survived into our own time." (Edward Lucie-Smith)

The puzzling question remains: how did so much modernist (and postmodernist) anti-art become legitimated as prized and highly-priced commodities?

This is the legitimation checkmate. The more experimentation successfully proceeds to **diminish** the aura and autonomy of art, the more aura and autonomy become the exclusive properties of **exhibitive power** - the critical establishment, curators, art-dealers and their clients.

Even the most outrageous anti-art cannot resist being **unwillingly** reproduced as "art" by the institutional powers of legitimation.

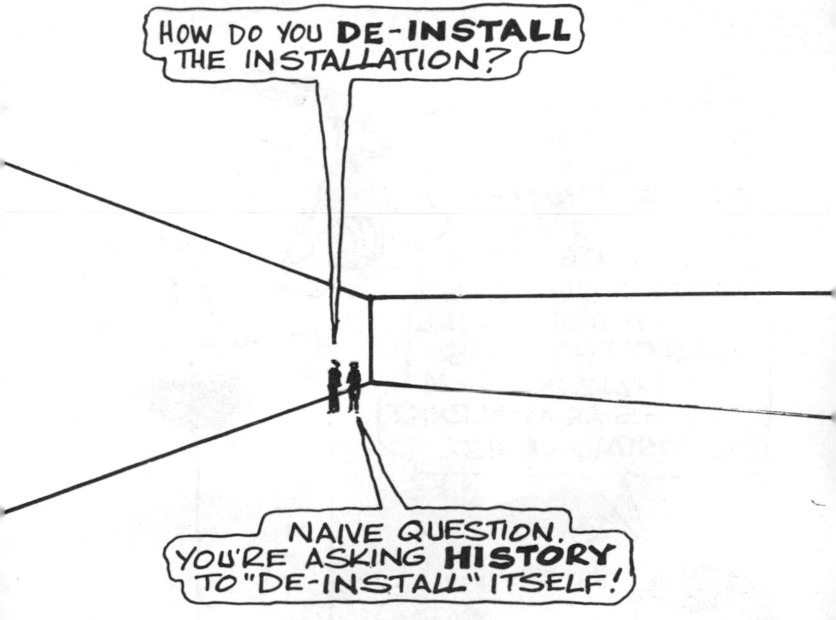

Early avantgarde modernists were naively utopian in expecting that history itself would confirm and legitimate their claims to represent "modernity" by attempting to invent it through **formalism** and **subversion**. Late (or post-) modernists are left with the legacy of formalist subversion - and a realization that the problems of **representation**, **reproduction** and **legitimation** are far more complex than were ever imagined by their predecessors.

The Simulacrum

It seems that the genealogy of postmodern art can only be disconnected from the modern **in theory.** Theory is not in this sense a culmination but a **negation**, literally, an "end of art." Let's look at the extreme postmodernist conclusion advanced by French sociologist Jean Baudrillard, that the representational image-sign goes through **4 successive historic phases...**

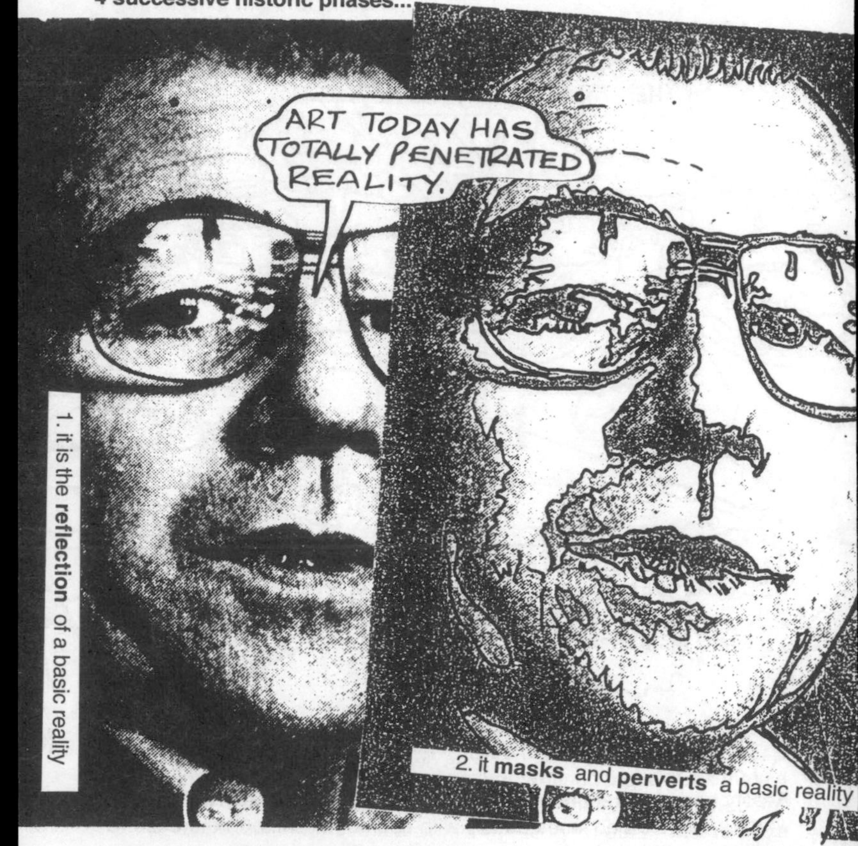

He means that the border between art and reality has utterly vanished as both have collapsed into the universal **simulacrum**.

The simulacrum is arrived at when the distinction between representation and reality - between signs and what they refer to in the real world - breaks down.

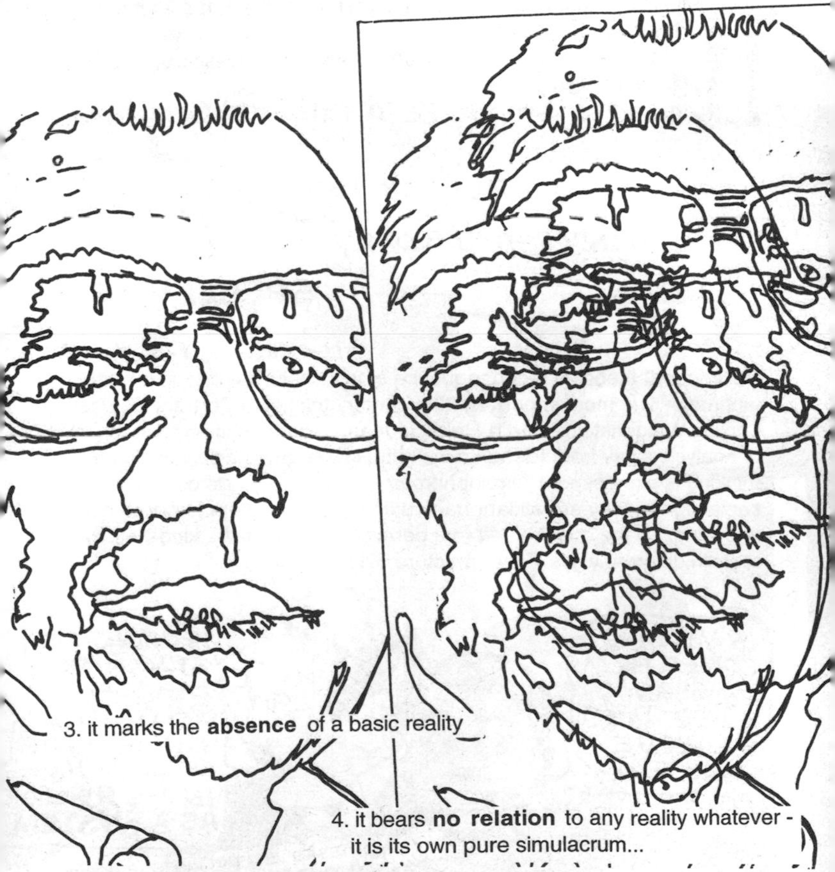
3. it marks the **absence** of a basic reality
4. it bears **no relation** to any reality whatever - it is its own pure simulacrum...

Reality becomes redundant and we have reached **hyper-reality** in which images breed incestuously with each other without reference to reality or meaning.
How is it possible to arrive at the **nullification** of reality, even "in theory"? And what is the **genealogy of a theory** that leads to such a radical conclusion?

PART TWO: THE GENEALOGY OF POSTMODERN THEORY

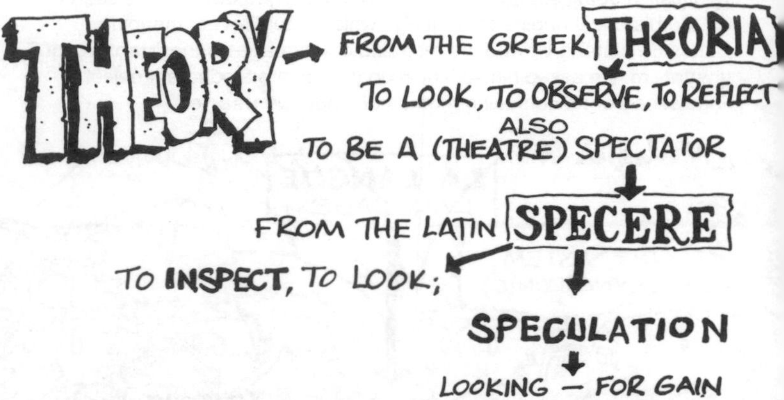
THEORY
FROM THE GREEK THEORIA
TO LOOK, TO OBSERVE, TO REFLECT
ALSO
TO BE A (THEATRE) SPECTATOR
FROM THE LATIN SPECERE
TO INSPECT, TO LOOK;
SPECULATION
LOOKING — FOR GAIN

Postmodern theory is a consequence of this century's obsession with language. The most important 20th century thinkers - Bertrand Russell, Ludwig Wittgenstein, Martin Heidegger and others - shifted their focus of analysis away from **ideas** in the mind to the **language** in which thinking is expressed. Philosophers or logicians, linguists or semiologists, they are all language detectives who seem to agree about one thing. To the question, "What permits meaningful thinking?", they reply in different ways, "The structure of language."

IF MEANING COMES FROM LANGUAGE, WHERE DOES LANGUAGE COME FROM?
FORGET THE ORIGIN OF LANGUAGE. YOU'LL FIND THE MEANING OF LANGUAGE IN ITS FUNCTION AS A SYSTEM.

Postmodern theory has its roots in one school of formal linguistics, **structuralism**, chiefly founded by a Swiss professor of linguistics, Ferdinand de Saussure (1857-1913).

Structuralism

Linguistics before Saussure tended to get bogged down in the search for the historical origins of language which would reveal meaning. Saussure instead viewed the meaning of language as the **function of a system**. He asked himself: how do you isolate a coherent object of linguistics from a confusing morass of language **usages**?

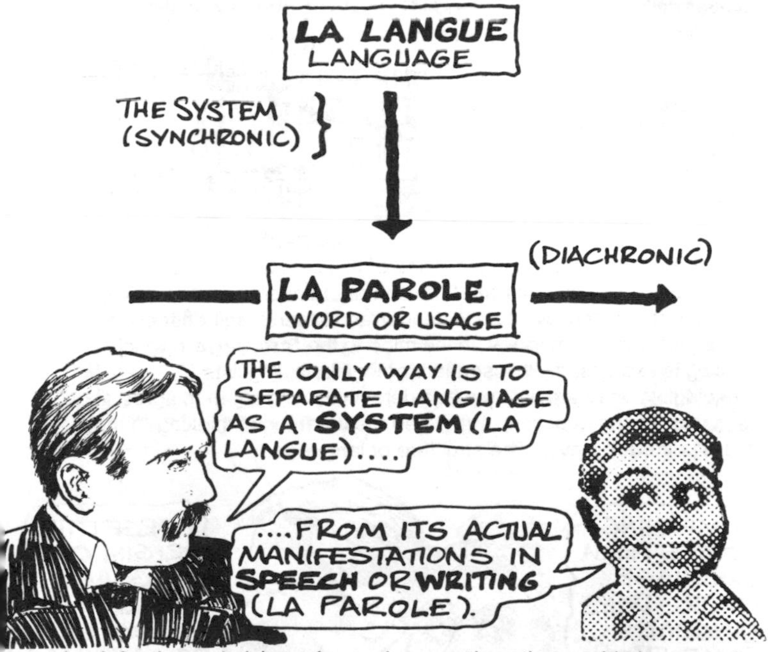

- Look for the underlying rules and conventions that enable language to operate.
- Analyze the social and collective dimension of language rather than individual speech.
- Study grammar rather than usage, rules rather than expressions, **models** rather than **data**.
- Find the infrastructure of language common to all speakers on an unconscious level. This is the "deep structure" which need not refer to historical evolution. Structuralism examines the **synchronic** (existing now) rather than the **diachronic** (existing and changing over time).

Meanings and Signs

In Saussure's view, the entire set of linguistic meanings (whether past, present or future) is effectively generated from a very small set of possible sounds or **phonemes**. A phoneme is the smallest unit in the sound system that can indicate contrasts in meaning. The word **cat** has 3 phonemes: /c/, /a/, /t/, which differ minimally from **mat,cot,cap,** etc., each generating other meanings that combined grammatically and syntactically can produce extended speech or **discourse**, the code of language used to express personal thought.

A DISTINCTION IS MADE BETWEEN **SIGNIFICANT UNITS**, –WORDS, OR *MONEMES*– EACH ONE ENDOWED WITH ONE "VALUE"...
...AND **DISTINCTIVE UNITS** – SOUNDS, OR *PHONEMES* – PART OF THE FORM BUT WITH NO DIRECT "VALUE".
A

Note the extreme economy of human language: with only 21 distinctive units American Spanish can produce 100,000 significant units.

Signification

Saussure proposed that within the language system, the **signifier** (e.g. the word or acoustic image, **ox**) is that which carries meaning, and the **signified** (the concept, **ox**) is that to which it refers.

Signifier and signified together } $\frac{Sr}{Sd}$ } make up a SIGN.

Signification is the process which binds together signifier and signified to produce the sign. A sign must be understood as a **relation** which has no meaning outside the system of signification.

The choice of sound is not imposed on us by meaning itself (the animal **ox** does not determine the sound **ox** - the sound is different in different languages: **ox** -English, **bue** - Italian).

The problem is - does the signified refer to the image or concept "ox" or to the ox **itself** as thing?
The association of sound and **what it represents** is the outcome of collective learning (use in social practice, or what Wittgenstein calls "language games") - and this is **signification**.
Meaning is therefore the product of a system of representation which is itself **meaningless**.

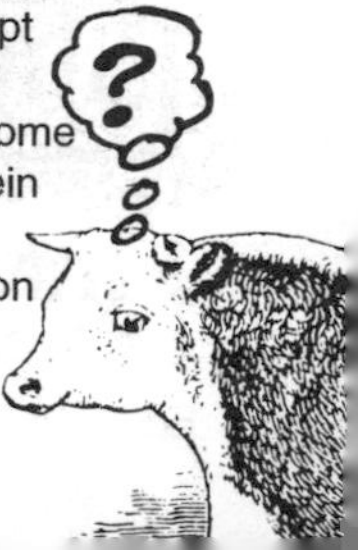

The Binary Model

Saussure bequeathed a decisive **binary model** to postmodern theory. Language is a sign system that functions by an operational code of **binary oppositions.** We have seen one binary opposition: Sr/Sd. Another crucial binary opposition is **syntagm/paradigm**, which operates as follows.

syntagmatic series (also called **contiguity** or **combination**) - the linear relationships between linguistic elements in a sentence

paradigmatic series (also called **selection** or **substitution**) - the relationship between elements within a sentence and other elements which are syntactically interchangeable

SYNTAGMATIC (COMBINATION)

He
shut
THE
door
SUBJECT, VERB AND OBJECT SYNTAGMATICALLY RELATED.

PARADIGMATIC (SUBSTITUTION)
WOULD YOU PLEASE MAKE UP YOUR MIND - IT'S FREEZING IN HERE!
He
shut
door
She
closed
window
They
opened
etc.
ARE PARADIGMATICALLY RELATED.

Figures of Speech: Metaphor and Metonymy

This apparently simple binary contrast of substitution and combination generates higher degrees of complexity and might be said to account for the imaginative or symbolic use of language - in other words, the possibility of meaningful **fictions**.

For instance: paradigmatic substitution involves a perception of **similarity** which can generate **METAPHOR** - "a tower of strength", "a glaring error" - descriptions that are not literally true.

Syntagmatic combination involves a perception of **contiguity** which can generate **METONYMY** (naming an attribute or adjunct of the thing instead of the thing itself - "crown" for royalty, "turf" for horse-racing) or **SYNECDOCHE** (naming the part for the whole - "keels" for ships).

Roman Jakobson (1895-1982), a Russian-born linguist, applied Saussure's binary model to **aphasia**, a severe speech disorder caused by brain damage. Jakobson identified two distinct kinds of aphasic disturbance.

Aphasics who suffer from (paradigmatic) substitution deficiency will resort to metonymic expressions.

Those deficient in (syntagmatic) combination are confined to using similarity or metaphor.

What does this tell us? There are two opposed forms of mental activity underlying the use of metaphor and metonymy.

In traditional literary criticism, metaphor and metonymy had always been thought of as related figures of speech. They are not related but opposed. The consequence of this is **extended discourses** in which either the metaphoric or metonymic order predominates...

METAPHORIC ORDER
PARADIGMATIC
SUBSTITUTION
SELECTION
POETRY
LYRICAL SONGS
ROMANTICISM
FILMIC
METAPHOR
SURREALISM

METONYMIC ORDER
SYNTAGMATIC
COMBINATION
CONTIGUITY
PROSE
HEROIC EPICS
War &
Peace
REALISM
Emile Zola
MONTAGE
in Croatia
raid is first
side Bosnia
JOURNALISM.

Semiology

Saussure and Jakobson's binary order has applications that extend into other "discourses" besides the text, and this is the domain of **semiology** (from the Greek **semeion**, a mark, sign, trace or omen).

Saussure opened the way to analyzing **culture** itself as a system of signs by proposing that structural linguistics was part of semiology, a general science of signs which studies the various systems of **cultural conventions** which enable human actions to signify meaning and hence **become** signs. Linguistics is a model of semiology because the arbitrary and conventional nature of language is especially clear.

Saussure's idea of semiology is this: the meaning of any action or object may seem natural, but is always founded on **shared conventions** (a system). Semiology avoids the usual mistake of assuming that signs which appear natural to their users must have "intrinsic" or "essential" meaning that requires no further explanation.

example: a restaurant menu

paradigmatic plane
a set of foodstuffs with affinities or differences from which "dishes" are chosen (metaphoric selection or substitution) in view of certain "meaning": types of hors d'oeuvres, entrées, roasts or sweets.
The sets of foodstuffs are the **signifiers**.

syntagmatic plane
real (metonymic or contiguous) sequence of dishes chosen during the meal.
The **signified** is the referent or cultural "value" - a meal.

Reading a menu **horizontally** (selection from the hors d'oeuvres) = the whole system.
Reading **vertically** (combining the menu sequence) = the syntagm.

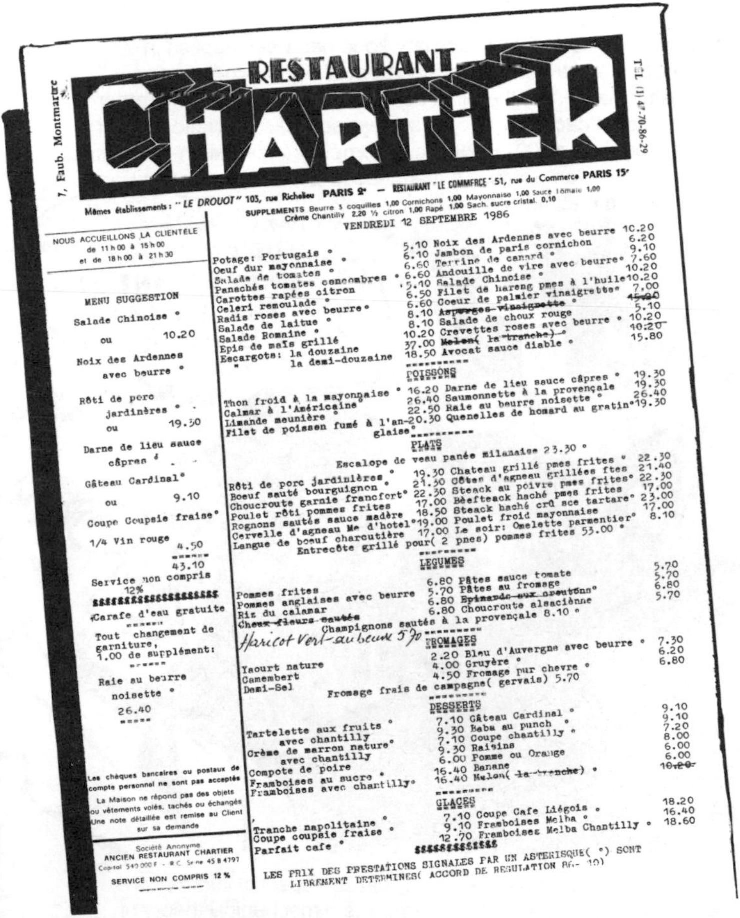

Semiology can be applied to decoding fashion, advertising, myth, architecture and so on.

Structural Anthropology

Claude Lévi-Strauss (b. 1908), following Saussure and the Slavic linguists Roman Jakobson and N.S. Trubetzkoy, developed **structural anthropology** in the late 1950s which systematized a semiology of culture.

At this time in the 1950s, the binary code had been applied in **cybernetics** and the rapid development of **digital computers.** Digitalism operates on the binary or base-number 2 system, rather than our usual decimal base 10 system and has a notation 1 and 0 (10 = 2, 1001 = 9, 11001 = 25, etc.). Computer information-processing operates on an "on" switch (a magnetized dot = 1) and "off" switch (absence of a magnetized dot = 0).

ANTHROPOLOGY IS A CULTURAL MODEL FOR UNDERSTANDING HOW THE HUMAN MIND UNIVERSALLY FUNCTIONS.

This technological binarism - the digitalized aspect of Information Theory - influenced Lévi-Strauss towards a mechanical theory of communication.
How does it work?

Language is the system that permits thinking. Thinking is the "system-output" that occurs in the interaction between human subjects (situated within culture) and the environment (nature) which is the object of thinking.

binarism

nature<-------------->culture
(non-human) (human)

Thinking can therefore occur because language allows us (1) to form **social relationships** and (2) to **categorize** our environment as represented by symbols.

Among many primitive peoples it is the custom for each tribe or family to adopt some object from Nature as their special symbol, or totem. This totem may be an animal or plant, or a carving in wood or stone, and is supposed to be helpful to the tribe it represents. Tribes which have an animal totem will never kill that special animal, while those that have adopted a plant as their symbol abstain from eating others of the same species. Poles surmounted by grotesque carvings are often set near the encampments of North American Indians as totems, while among the aborigines of Australia totemism is almost universal.
THIS TRADITIONALIST, EUROCENTRIC VIEW IS MISLEADING...
TOTEMISM IS NOT SOME BIZARRE 'PRIMITIVE' SUPERSTITION, BUT A BASIC INSTANCE OF LOGIC. IT IS THINKING.

Totems are categories that specify (divide up) what's "out there" as symbols for thinking, in other words, binary classifications.

What can or cannot be eaten (and why).
Who can or cannot be married (and why).

Thinking in this sense is literally (re)**producing society**.

How is the binarism **human/ non-human** reflected in totemism?

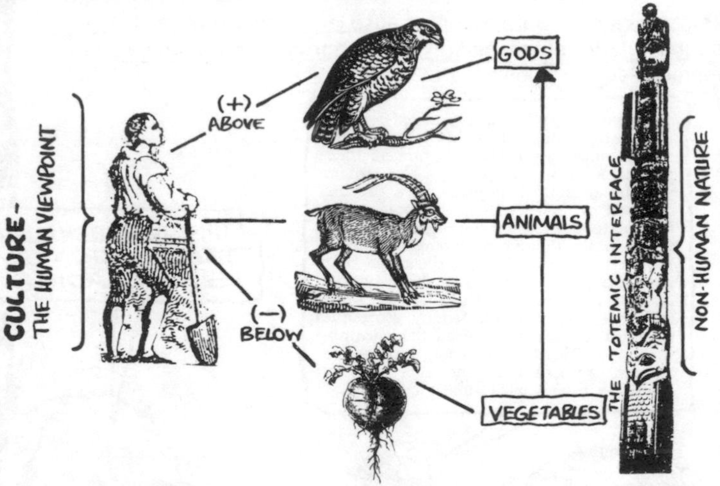

Tribal societies apply **substitutions** (metaphors) and **combinations** (metonyms) to "think" about non-human nature. Animals and vegetables aren't simply things to eat but are **read as codes** that link nature to human society by way of the "higher" (non-human) gods. This is a code-chain that runs two ways.

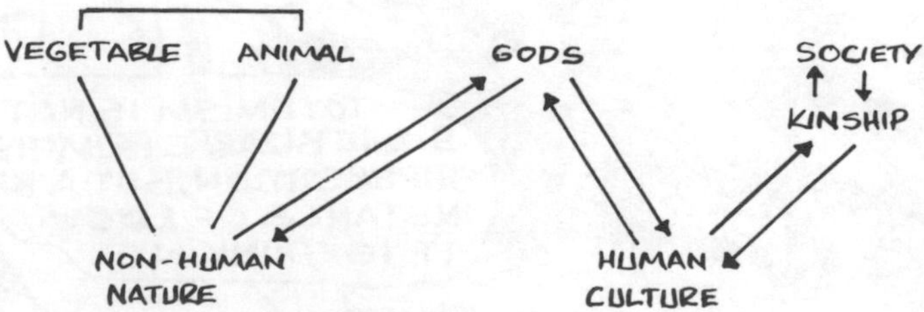

The human mind functions in model binary sets - noise/silence, raw/cooked, naked/clothed, light/darkness, sacred/profane and so on.

Minds working logically (that is **culturally**) unconsciously duplicate nature. An example. Why have we chosen the colours green, yellow and red for our traffic-light sign system?
Because it is a "fact of nature" that our colour code signals for **Go - Caution - Stop** mimick the same structure found in the spectrum.

Green is a short wavelength, red is long and yellow lies midway.

The brain searches for a **representation** of the binary opposition (go) +/- (stop), and finds green and red and also the intermediate colour term (/) caution, yellow.

Brief Critique of Structuralism

The positive benefits of structuralist analysis are undeniable. But so are its negative shortcomings.

1. Dematerialization and formalism

Saussure's language system eliminates **material origins**; it also **de**-psychologizes, since it need not posit an "unconscious" motivation even on a biological level.

Although Saussure speaks of "deep structures", these have nothing to do with the unconscious in a Freudian sense. Structuralist analysis is an abstract "surface" reading as opposed to a Marxian or Freudian "deep" reading which thinks in terms of **symptoms** - origins, causes and cures. In contrast, structuralism is value-free of such "medical" ambitions.

Similarly, although Jakobson does not deny the material (neurological) origin and reality of aphasia, his analysis tends to de-materialize and formalize it.

Structuralism opens out a formal area of inquiry - a non-dimensional space of abstraction - which might seem to resemble philosophy ("thinking about thinking") and its exclusive reliance on the **rules** of reasoning to arrive at a general picture of the world.

Structuralism goes much further in the direction of **hyper-rationalism**. It claims that "meaning" is a product of signification, a process maintained by timeless and universal structures forming a stable and self-contained system based on binary oppositions. The elements of the system, or signifiers, carry meaning only in relation to each other; their relationship to the signified - whether concepts or things or actions - is arbitrary, based purely on convention.

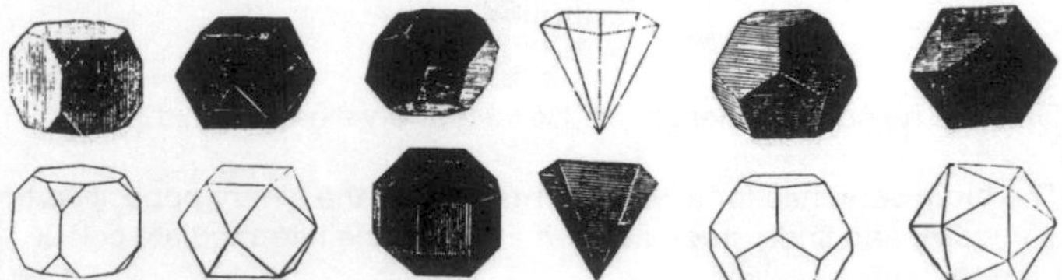

2. Formalizing the human

"I think therefore I am." What happens to this famous Cartesian proof of self-identity in the structuralist view?
The "I" or unitary human subject - the very cornerstone of Western logic and philosophy - dissolves into a **signifying language-user**. The "I" is a language fiction, signified by **use**, not **meaning**, and generated in much the same way as metaphor or metonymy.

Structuralism is unhelpful in explaining what **motivates** the language-using subject, i.e., the individual.

The logic of the system entirely surpasses and evades the subject's **reasons** for using language. Saying, "to communicate his personal thought", is not good enough. How did "personal thought" get into the system, anyhow? can there even be personal thought in such a structured/closed system?

3. Non-historical

Structuralism is non-historical, or more accurately, **a**-historical. Its analysis is valid (in principle) no matter what is historically present. This is consistent with its discarding of historical origins and motivations.
These features of structuralism's rigorous abstract intellectuality mark it as a typically modernist project - and yet as an instant flip-over into postmodern theory. As we noted before, "modern must inevitably become **post**modern".

We can witness this happening by seeing what actually happened to structuralism in its own heyday in the 1960s.

Poststructuralism

We can see the beginnings of a po mo attitude in the mid-60s with the overlap of structuralism and the "post"-structuralist second thoughts of **Roland Barthes** (1915-80).

...WE MUST NOW FACE THE POSSIBILITY OF INVERTING SAUSSURE'S DECLARATION: LINGUISTICS IS NOT A PART OF THE GENERAL SCIENCE OF SIGNS, EVEN A PRIVILEGED PART, IT IS SEMIOLOGY WHICH IS PART OF LINGUISTICS...
..ARE YOU WARM, ARE YOU REAL, MONA LISA....?

Barthes is saying that semiological analysis **collapses back** into language - a forerunner of Baudrillard's more radical notion of "art totally penetrating reality", of the border between art and reality vanishing as the two collapse into the universal simulacrum. A collapse into **total semblance.**

Barthes in the mid-60s doesn't go quite so far - but almost. He notes that semiology itself can be added to Jakobson's classification of **metaphoric types**, along with lyrical songs, Chaplin's films and Surrealism. Barthes explicitly states...

"The metalanguage in which the semiologist conducts his analysis is **metaphorical**..."

Barthes is (partly) responding to a higher degree of **reflexivity**, a typically postmodern penance paid for modernist intellectual arrogance.

Reflexivity doesn't mean simply to "reflect on" (which usually comes later, or too late) but is an immediate critical consciousness of what one is doing, thinking or writing. However, since it is impossible to do anything innocently in our age of lost innocence, reflexivity can easily slide into ironic self-consciousness, cynicism and politically correct hypocrisy.

the completely genuine: the completely human

The Death of the Author

Barthes was an early and elegant exponent of semiotics who recognized that anything in culture can be decoded - not just literature but fashion, wrestling, strip tease, steak and chips, love, photography and even Japan Incorporated.

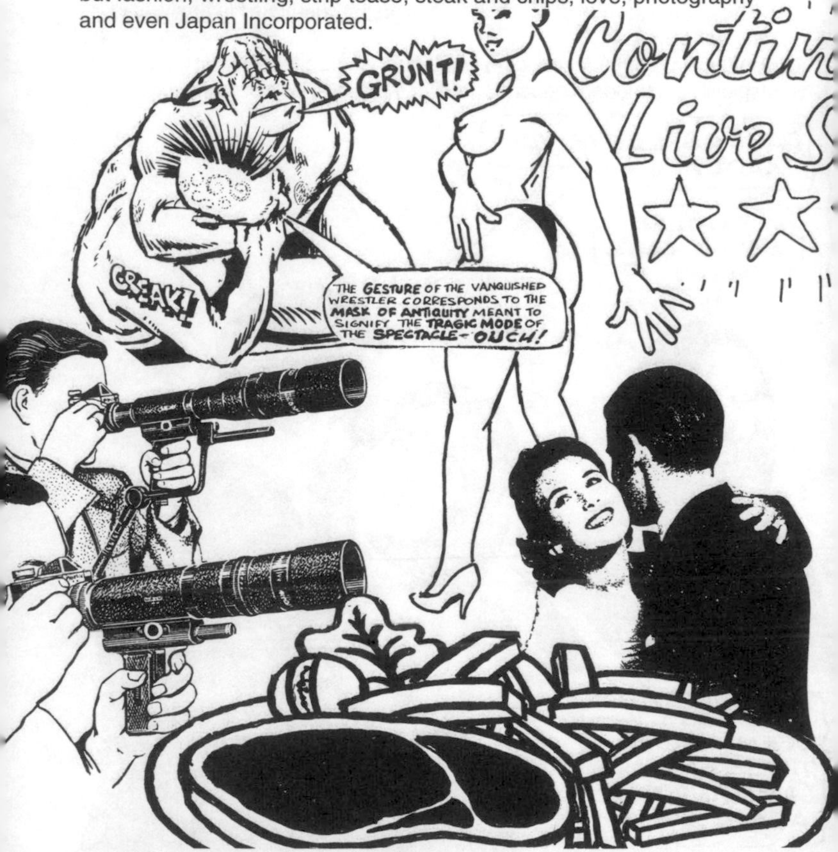
GRUNT!
CREAK!
THE GESTURE OF THE VANQUISHED WRESTLER CORRESPONDS TO THE MASK OF ANTIQUITY MEANT TO SIGNIFY THE TRAGIC MODE OF THE SPECTACLE - OUCH!

In 1967, Barthes caused a sensation by proclaiming "the death of the author". He meant that readers create their own meanings, regardless of the author's intentions: the texts they use to do so are thus ever-shifting, unstable and open to question. This applies equally to the scientific or structuralist author who cannot stand outside such interpretation.

Writing: Degree Zero

Unstable interpretations are inevitable because writing tends to a "zero degree" of sense. What does Barthes mean?

YOU CAN READ A TEXT FOR PLEASURE AND SENSE... BUT YOU'RE FINALLY LEFT WITH A SENSE OF ENIGMA, A **FINAL** SENSE WHICH THE TEXT DOESN'T EXPRESS OR REFUSES TO SURRENDER— A SORT OF UNYIELDING **THOUGHTFULNESS**. IT IS LIKE THE THOUGHTFULNESS OF A FACE WHICH TEMPTS ONE TO ASK..."WHAT ARE YOU THINKING?"

.....OR JUST A COLD AND LONELY, LOVELY WORK OF ART?

IM THINKING IT'S ABOUT TIME YOU GOT ME ANOTHER DRINK.

This is the zero degree of writing - a closure, a retreat and a suspension of meaning.

...Poststructuralist Blues...

No Exit from Language

HOW FAR HAVE WE GOT WITH RESOLVING THE BIG 3 PROBLEMS- -REPRESENTATION REPRODUCTION AND LEGITIMATION?
FAR ENOUGH TO BE DISILLUSIONED WITH META-LANGUAGES TO RESOLVE THEM.

A **metalanguage** is a technical language, such as structuralism, devised to describe the properties of ordinary language. Wittgenstein had already come up against the limits of logic as a metalanguage in the 1920s.

YOU CAN'T STAND OUTSIDE LANGUAGE TO UNDERSTAND IT.

A privileged or "meta"-linguistic position is a mirage created by language itself. Structuralism, semiology and other forms of metalinguistics which promised liberation from the enigma of meaning, only lead back to language, a no exit, and the consequent dangers of a relativist or even nihilistic view of human reason itself. **Deconstruction**, an offshoot of poststructuralism, has often been accused of "relativizing everything". What is deconstruction?

Deconstruction

One of the most influencial postmoderns, the philosopher Jacques Derrida (b.1930) has waged a one-man "deconstructionist" war against the entire Western tradition of rationalist thought. In particular, Derrida has targeted Western philosophy's central assumption of **Reason** which he sees as dominated by a "metaphysics of presence".

WHAT'S WRONG WITH REASON? AND WHAT'S IT GOT TO DO WITH PRESENCE?
REASON HAS BEEN SHAPED BY A DISHONEST PURSUIT OF CERTAINTY WHICH I HAVE DIAGNOSED AS LOGOCENTRICISM – THE GUARANTEE OF "THE WORD MADE FLESH".
In the beginning was the WORD, and the Word was with God, and the Word was God... and the Word was made flesh, and dwelt among us...
JOHN I: 1–14
The Sleep of Reason

The history of philosophy from Plato, its founding father, and Aristotle, Kant, Hegel, right up to Wittgenstein and Heidegger, has been a constant logocentric quest. Logocentricism derives from the Greek **logos**, "the word by which the inward thought is expressed" or "reason itself".

J'ACCUSE!

Logocentricism desires a perfectly rational language that perfectly represents the real world. Such a language of reason would absolutely guarantee that the **presence** of the world - the essence of **everything** in the world - would be transparently (re)**present**(ed) to an observing subject who could speak of it with complete certainty. Words would literally be the Truth of things - the "Word made flesh", as St. John puts it.

Pure communion with the world - that is the seduction of logocentric Reason.

Derrida is outraged by the totalitarian arrogance implicit in the claims of Reason. His anger does not seem so eccentric when we recall the shameful history of atrocities committed by rationalist Western cultures - the systematic "rationality" of mass extermination in the Nazi era, the scientific rationalism of the A-bomb and the Hiroshima holocaust....

Against the essentialist notion of certainty of meaning, Derrida mobilizes the central insight of structuralism - that meaning is not inherent in signs, nor in what they refer to, but results purely from the relationships between them. He draws out the radical "post-structuralist" implications of this point - that structures of meaning (without which nothing exists for us) include and **implicate** any observers of them. To observe is to interact, so the "scientific" detachment of structuralists or of any other rationalist position is untenable.

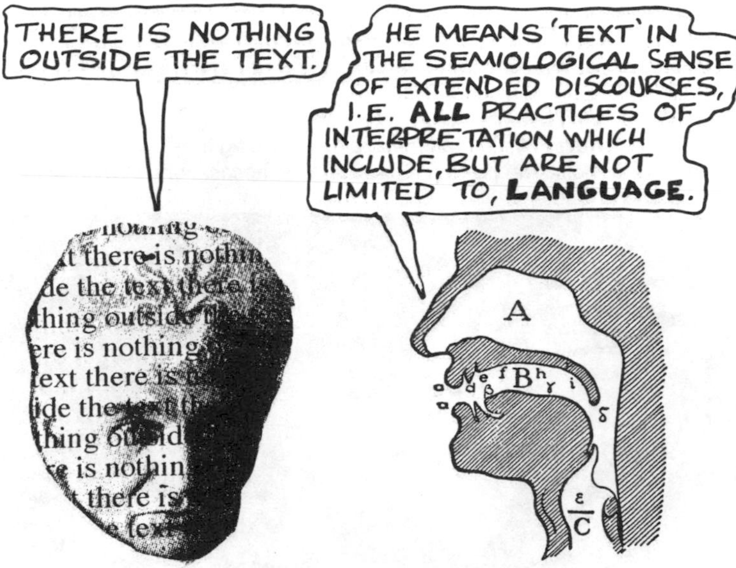
THERE IS NOTHING OUTSIDE THE TEXT.
HE MEANS 'TEXT' IN THE SEMIOLOGICAL SENSE OF EXTENDED DISCOURSES, I.E. **ALL** PRACTICES OF INTERPRETATION WHICH INCLUDE, BUT ARE NOT LIMITED TO, **LANGUAGE**.
A
B
C

Structuralism's insight to this extent was correct. It was incorrect to suppose that anything **reasoned** is ever universal, timeless and stable. Any meaning or identity (including our own) is provisional and relative, because it is **never exhaustive**, it can always be traced further back to a prior network of differences, and further back again...almost to infinity or the "zero degree" of sense. This is **deconstruction** - to peel away like an onion the layers of constructed meanings.

"Différance"

Deconstruction is a strategy for revealing the underlayers of meanings "in" a text that were suppressed or assumed in order for it to take its actual form - in particular the assumptions of "presence" (the hidden representations of guaranteed certainty).

Texts are never simply unitary but include resources that run counter to their assertions and/ or their authors' intentions.

Meaning includes identity (what it is) and difference (what it isn't) and it is therefore continuously being "deferred". Derrida invented a word for this process, combining difference and deferral - **différance**.

Derrida has tried to extract a positive benefit from the disillusioning failure of a structuralist metalanguage by upholding its subversive merits. In so doing, he has left himself open to accusations of relativism and irrationalism.

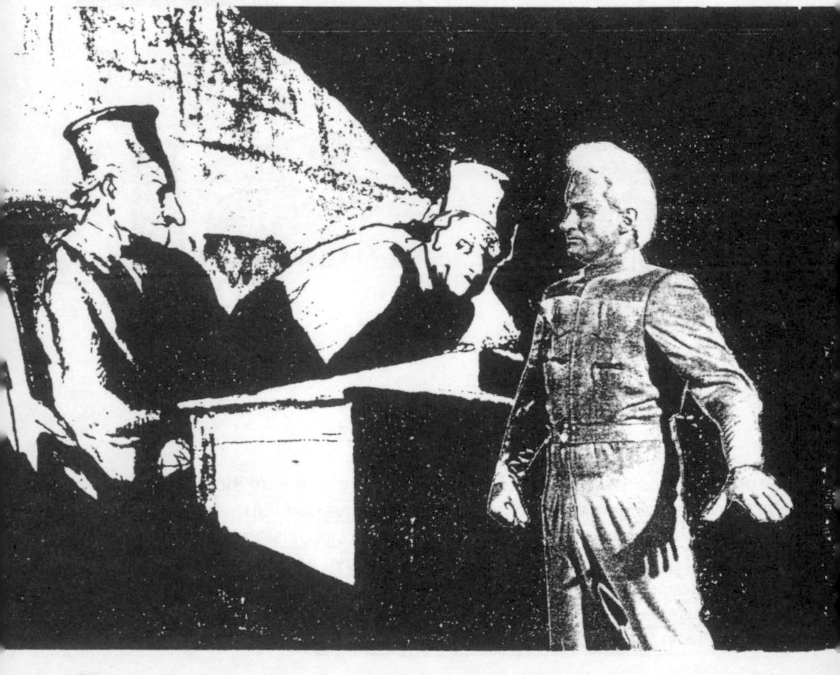

The Accuser Accused...

YOU REJECT REASON.
NO... ONLY ITS DOGMATIC REPRES-ENTATION OF ITSELF AS TIMELESS CERTAINTY.
YOU SAY NOTHING IS REAL BECAUSE EVERYTHING IS ONLY A CULTURAL, LINGUISTIC OR HISTORICAL CONSTRUCT.
NOTHING IS ANY LESS REAL FOR BEING CULTURAL, LINGUISTIC OR HISTORICAL, ESPECIALLY IF THERE IS NO UNIVERSAL OR TIMELESS REALITY TO WHICH IT CAN BE COMPARED. - ANYTHING ELSE?
YOU SAY THERE ARE AN INFINITE NUMBER OF MEANINGS.
NO - ONLY THAT THERE IS NEVER JUST ONE.
YOU SAY EVERYTHING IS OF EQUAL VALUE.
NO. ONLY THAT THE QUESTION MUST REMAIN OPEN.

The Structures of Power/Knowledge

The historian Michel Foucault (1926-84) is the postmodern theorist most directly concerned with the problems of power and legitimation. He tackles power from the unusual angle of **knowledge** as systems of thought which become controlling, that is, socially legitimated and institutional. Foucault initially called his investigations of knowledge an "archaeology" of **epistemes** (from the Greek **epistomai**, "to understand, to know for certain, to believe", which gives us **epistemology**, the verification theory of knowledge concerned with distinguishing genuine from spurious knowledge).

Foucault's episteme is a system of possible discourse which "somehow" comes to dominate each historical era. He concentrates on the "somehow" by which an episteme dictates what counts as knowledge and truth and what doesn't.

THE CRITERIA OF EPISTEMES CAN BE DEFINED THROUGH WHAT, OR WHOM, THEY EXCLUDE OR DISQUALIFY. IN THE CASE OF MODERNITY – THE MAD, THE SICK AND THE CRIMINAL....

Foucault completely upsets our conventional expectations of history as something linear - a chronology of inevitable facts that tell a story which makes sense. Instead, he uncovers the underlayers of what is kept suppressed and unconscious **in** and **throughout** history - the codes and assumptions of order, the structures of exclusion that legitimate the epistemes, by which societies achieve their identities.

THERE IS NO "HISTORY" BUT A MULTIPLE, OVERLAPPING AND INTERACTIVE SERIES OF LEGITIMATE Vs. EXCLUDED HISTORIES.

By the mid-70s,
Foucault moved away from "archaeology" towards the "genealogy" of what he now called "power/knowledge" and he focused more on the "microphysics" of how power moulds everyone (and not only its victims) involved in its exercise. He showed how power and knowledge fundamentally depend on each other, so that the extension of one is simultaneously the extension of the other. In so doing, the reason of rationalism requires - even creates - social categories of the mad, criminal and deviant against which to define itself. It is thus sexist, racist and imperialist in practice.

Art and Power/Knowledge

Literature and art are closely linked to knowledge in Foucault's view of history, not situated within the episteme but rather articulating its limits. Art is **meta-epistemic**: it is **about** the episteme as a whole, an allegory of the deep arrangements that make knowledge possible.
An example. Suppose Foucault were looking at Picasso's **Demoiselles d'Avignon**; what would his archaeology make of the "deformed" nude prostitutes on show?
There are structural disparities to consider.

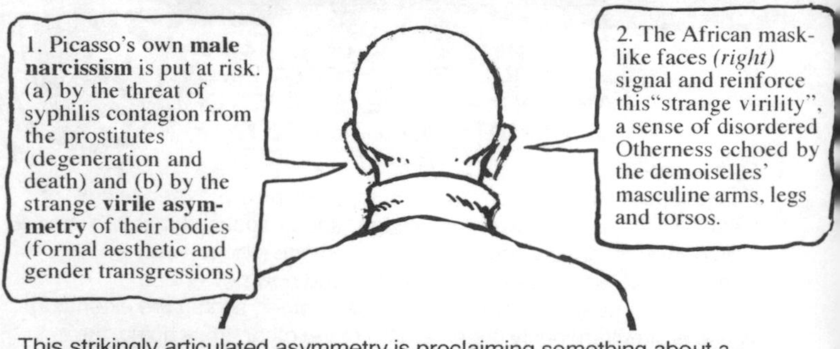
1. Picasso's own **male narcissism** is put at risk. (a) by the threat of syphilis contagion from the prostitutes (degeneration and death) and (b) by the strange **virile asymmetry** of their bodies (formal aesthetic and gender transgressions)
2. The African mask-like faces *(right)* signal and reinforce this"strange virility", a sense of disordered Otherness echoed by the demoiselles' masculine arms, legs and torsos.

This strikingly articulated asymmetry is proclaiming something about a **social category of exclusion**.
What is it?

Eugenics: measuring the excluded inferior

Fear of racial degeneration in Western societies marked the early 1900s, a danger posed by the epidemic consequences of syphilis, but especially by the threat of **criminal sub-types**.
Eugenics, a pseudo-science of "racial improvement" based on Darwin's idea of natural selection, drew on the new sciences of neurology, psychiatry and anthropology to distinguish the fit from the unfit. **Anthropometrics** (an applied branch of physical anthropology) measured the shapes of countless heads, noses, ears and limbs to classify the ideally proportioned (healthy/superior) human types and the degenerate sub-types. In the sub-types belonged the savage (non-European) races, the insane, criminals and prostitutes, all classifiable by **asymmetrical features**.

included (FIT) humans

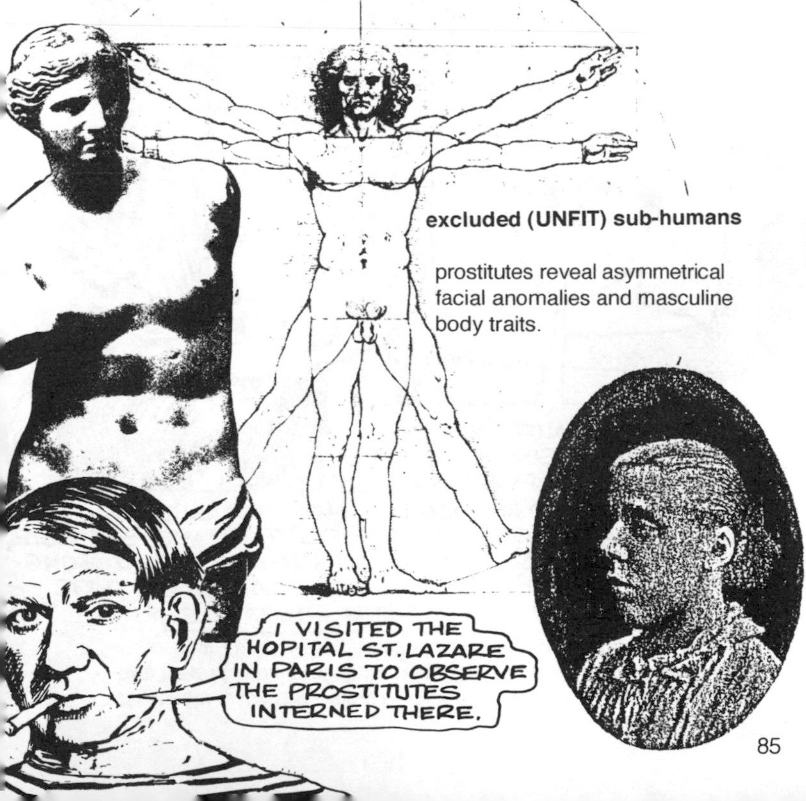
excluded (UNFIT) sub-humans
prostitutes reveal asymmetrical facial anomalies and masculine body traits.
I VISITED THE HOPITAL ST. LAZARE IN PARIS TO OBSERVE THE PROSTITUTES INTERNED THERE.

Some possible conclusions

-Racialist eugenics is an essential component of modernity's **episteme** - its system of dominant knowledge - which leads to Nazism's Final Solution by mass extermination of "unfit types".
-Picasso's painting is **meta-epistemic**: it disturbingly allegorizes the whole episteme by including what it excludes.
-It is "about" the problem of representation in modernity - how knowledge of the Self and Other is constituted, reproduced and legitimated.

Avantgarde modern art which supposedly begins with Picasso's **Demoiselles d'Avignon** can be seen as originating in protest and **reaction against** the unlimited totalizing project of modern rationalism.

What is Power?

Power cannot only be coercive. It also has to be productive and enabling.

POWER WOULD BE A FRAGILE THING IF ITS ONLY FUNCTION WERE TO **REPRESS.**

Foucault criticized the Marxist-Freudian liberation model of sexuality as a natural instinct repressed by authoritarian familial and social institutions.

IT IS NOT SIMPLY A MATTER OF DISCOVERING THE 'TRUTH' ABOUT OUR REPRESSED DESIRES BY EMBRACING A MODEL OF LIBERATION. THE PROBLEM IS - HOW DO PEOPLE BECOME SUBJECT TO A PARTICULAR KIND OF SEXUAL ***EXPERIENCE?***

How is an "experience" articulated in a system of rules and constraints so that we can recognize ourselves as subjects of a sexuality which opens into optional fields of knowledge?

Foucault is saying that power isn't what some possess and others don't, but a tactical and resourceful **narrative**. Power is in the texture of our lives - we **live** it rather than **have** it.

The Fiction of the Self

French psychoanalyst **Jacques Lacan** (1901-81) led a "back to Freud" movement after being himself expelled from the orthodox International Psychoanalytical Association. Lacan's notoriously obscure writing is modelled on the arcane style of the French Symbolist poet Stéphane Mallarmé (1842-98) and also harks back to wilful Surrealist provocation (some of his early work in the 1930s appeared in the Surrealist journal **Minotaure**).

THE UNCONSCIOUS IS STRUCTURED AS A LANGUAGE.
THIS IS LACAN'S MOST FAMOUS PRONOUNCE-MENT. WHAT DOES IT MEAN? HOW CAN THE UNCONSCIOUS, WHICH IS INSTINCTUAL AND, BY DEFINITION, UNKNOWABLE TO THE SUBJECT, BE STRUCTURED AS A LANGUAGE?

Whereas Freud keeps faith with a materialist biology of mind, Lacan applies Saussure's linguistics to explain how the mind comes to be structured and inserted in a social order.

Lacan replaces Freud's classic trinity of the psyche - Id, Ego and Superego - with structures of the **Imaginary**, the **Symbolic** and the **Real** which represent the stages of human psychic maturation.

THE UNCONSCIOUS FUNCTIONS BY SIGNS, METAPHORS, SYMBOLS, AND IN THIS SENSE IT IS "LIKE" A LANGUAGE.
BUT LACAN'S POINT IS THAT THE UNCONSCIOUS ONLY COMES TO EXIST **AFTER** LANGUAGE IS ACQUIRED.

The Imaginary or "Mirror Phase"

Between 6 to 18 months, the infant makes its first startling discovery of itself in the mirror as an image which appears total and coherent.

THE INFANT IMAGINARY PHASE PRECEDES LANGUAGE AND CONTRIBUTES TO THE WAY WE ACQUIRE IT.

A sense of self arrives externally, from a **reflection**, or from the imaginary. Identity comes from **mis**-recognition, a false persuasion of Self, which remains with us as an ideal ego for the rest of our lives. The mirror supplies the first **Signified** and the infant itself acts as the **Signifier**.

Lacan is saying that we are all imprisoned not in reality but in a hall-of-mirrors world of signifiers

The Symbolic Order

The Symbolic order refers to the system of pre-existing social structures into which the child is born, such as kinship, rituals, gender roles and indeed language itself.

Identity assumed at the Imaginary phase is finally constructed by the Symbolic order, the realm of the Father who prohibits the mother-child "incest" relationship.

Language belongs to the Father, that is, to the patriarchal order of the **phallus**.

The male child resolves his Oedipal "murderous" conflict with the Father by identifying with Phallic Power.

He can do this because he possesses a "signifier" - his penis - which in the Signified realm represents the Phallus or Sexual Power.

The position of power in language **is** the Phallus which imposes the Symbolic order.

-AND WOMEN?
THEY ARE EXCLUDED - FOREVER OUTCAST AS "THE OTHERS" - WITHOUT LANGUAGE BECAUSE THEY CANNOT ESCAPE FROM THE IMAGINARY INTO THE SYMBOLIC ORDER, AS MALES CAN.

Patriarchy silences women.

Not entirely silenced...

Paradoxically, Lacan's extreme marginalization of women has given a boost to postmodern feminist theory.

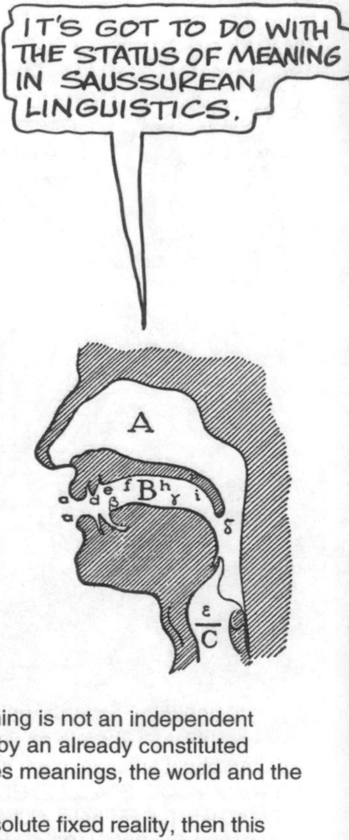

Remember, structuralism says that meaning is not an independent representation of the real world grasped by an already constituted subject, but part of a system that produces meanings, the world and the **possibility of a subject**.

If identity is a construction and not an absolute fixed reality, then this opens up immense scope for feminist thinking. The entire historical process by which identity has been represented as a self-evident certainty is thrown into question. Derrida's attack on logocentric certainty, Foucault's unveiling of historical exclusion and Lacan's own idea of the self as fiction can be seen as weapons useful to postmodern feminism.

No Place in History

Let's look at two examples of postmodern feminism, beginning with **Luce Irigaray** (b. Belgium, 1932).

WOMEN HAVE BEEN ASSIGNED NO PLACE IN HISTORY. JUST LOOK AT THE WAY WOMEN HAVE BEEN REPRESENTED...
ONLY BY METONYMY DO I EXIST AS A POSSIBILITY FOR MEN.

They appear as **exterior** representations either of **something else** - monuments of Justice, Liberty, Peace....
or as **objects of men's desire**.

Woman is represented by a form of metonymic **differentiation** that reproduces her oppression by excluding her from history.

WOMEN HAVE BEEN PUT IN THE SCHIZOID POSITION OF BEING SIMULTANEOUSLY ***IN*** HISTORY AND ***NOT*** IN HISTORY — "WRITTEN OUT" OF HISTORY BY MALE THEORY.

Male theories of sexuality - Freud's or Lacan's - literally cannot **think** of women except as negatively imaginary, incomplete, an empty signifier (the vacant womb).

Women are the sex which isn't one.

THAT LEAVES ONLY TWO POSSIBILITIES...

EITHER - there is no feminine sexuality except as men imagine it
OR - feminine sexuality is a schizoid duality

(a) subordinate to the needs and desires of men
(b) autonomous and explorable only within a radically **separatist** women's movement

As a result of these views, the psychoanalyst Irigaray was expelled from the Lacanian psychoanalytical school in 1974.

Julia Kristeva (b. Bulgaria, 1941), a pioneer semiotician and psychoanalyst, agrees with Irigaray in refuting the Freudian and Lacanian accounts of identity which place the feminine outside the process of self-constitution. Meaning is not a once-and-for-all break from the Unconscious which occurs when the signifying subject enters the Symbolic order. Although it can never be "spoken", the Unconscious is the biological preliminary to meaning, its uterus, which always remains present as a force that can disrupt signification.

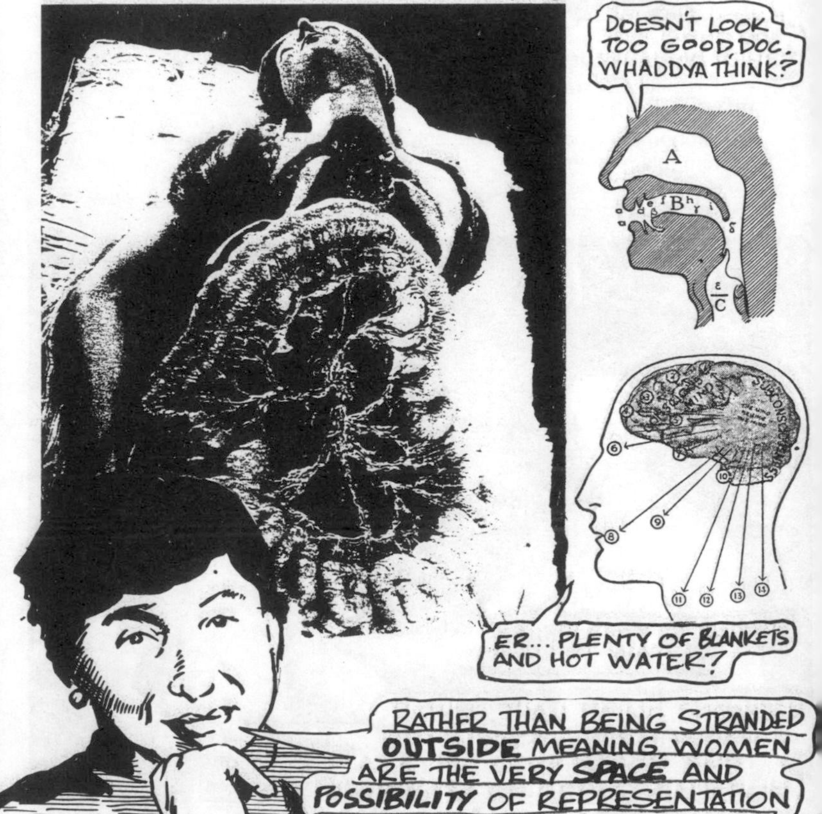

Kristeva places the semiotic in the Unconscious pre-Oedipal stage as that which both **withholds** and **permits** meaning which can de-stabilize the dominant repressive discourse of the Symbolic order.

Kristeva goes to an extreme in rejecting the category itself of "woman". She refuses to believe in an "essential" woman, a fixed gender, and tries to project a Subject beyond the categories of gender.
She is impatient with liberal emancipatory feminism, asserting that the main egalitarian demands of the past have been largely met.

THE VERY DICHOTOMY MAN/WOMAN AS AN OPPOSITION BETWEEN TWO RIVAL ENTITIES MAY BE UNDERSTOOD AS BELONGING TO METAPHYSICS. WHAT CAN "IDENTITY"– EVEN "SEXUAL IDENTITY"– MEAN IN A NEW THEORETICAL AND SCIENTIFIC SPACE, WHERE THE VERY **NOTION** OF IDENTITY IS CHALLENGED?
X366
SEARCH ME, MS. KRISTEVA, I'M JUST THE PILOT.

Kristeva has been much criticized by "egalitarian" feminists for soft-pedalling the real misery which sexual difference still causes for women, and therefore neutralizing women's real experience. She is seen as in danger of sending women back to "loving maternity".

What is Postmodern Feminism?

Feminism's position in so-called postmodernity highlights the artificially constructed debate between "modernism" and "postmodernism". This debate has served to divide liberal (modernist) feminism from radical (postmodern) feminism.

Liberal feminism is deep-rooted in modernity. It is a **rationalist** project of emancipation, originally inspired by the ideals of revolutionary Enlightenment in America and France, and classically formulated by Mary Wollstonecraft's **Vindication of the Rights of Women** in 1792.

Wollstonecraft imagined that the rights of men, enshrined in the American Declaration of Independence, could be extended to women without causing large-scale disruptions to the existing social institutions.

Militant feminism since Wollstonecraft's day came to recognize a dilemma that is still unresolved.

EITHER - coexist **with** men on the liberal route to egalitarianism
OR - come out **against** men on a radical separatist route

The second route has been defined by women's communalism, radical lesbianism and Andrea Dworkin's extreme formulation of men as all essentially rapists. But both routes are inherently modernist and do not constitute an opposition between modern-versus-postmodern. Postmodernism comes in only with a deconstructionist notion of a Subject beyond the fixed categories of gender. A **third term** is introduced. As Kristeva says...

Such an idea becomes possible if a certain model of historical progress is rejected, as we'll next see...

The end of the story...

Emancipationist political activity of any kind depends on a model of linear **purposeful** time in which the historical achievements of one generation are passed on to the next. This is the modernist model of history in which deliberate acts of self-assertion progress towards the realization of a distantly idealized goal.

Marxism is the classic example of a long-term emancipationist goal guaranteed by history itself.

SUPPOSE IT IS A DELUSION?..
The credit - or the blame - goes to Jean-François Lyotard for replying:
BUT THEN, WHAT HAS SUSTAINED THE DELUSION FOR SO LONG?

The liberation of humanity is a self-legitimizing myth, a “Grand Narrative” or **metanarrative**, maintained ever since the Enlightenment succeeded in turning philosophy into militant politics.

Lyotard has defined the postmodern condition as "scepticism towards all metanarratives". Metanarratives are the supposedly universal, absolute or ultimate truths that are used to legitimize various projects, political or scientific. Examples are: the emancipation of humanity through that of the workers (Marx); the creation of wealth (Adam Smith); the evolution of life (Darwin); the dominance of the unconscious mind (Freud), and so on.

Lyotard prescribed this scepticism in 1979, ten years before the Berlin Wall came tumbling down - and almost overnight the world witnessed the total collapse of a Socialist Grand Narrative...

The collapse of so-called "really existing" Socialism in Eastern Europe gave final proof that postmodern scepticism was preferable to modernist hyper-rationalism.

It justified Kristeva's claim in 1981...

History, Future, Identity, truth, Self are simply **not** things.

ANY RATIONALIST ATTEMPT TO TRANSFORM THE WORLD INTO ITS OWN IMAGE IS ONLY ONE MORE INTERPRETATION WHICH CANNOT SEE THAT IT EMBRACES A **VOID**.

For Lyotard, the decline and fall of modernist Grand Narratives was inevitable because of an absolutely decisive shift in **knowledge** itself. What does he mean by this?

SCIENCE IS NOT BEYOND THE REACH OF THE POSTMODERN QUESTION — WHAT MAKES IT **LEGITIMATE**?

Scientific Legitimation

Lyotard confronted another metanarrative myth (besides the one of political emancipation) which legitimized a modernist view of science. This is the "speculative unity of all knowledge", the goal of German Romantic philosophy maximized by the idealist metaphysics of **G.W.F. Hegel** (1770-1831).

This dream, exemplified by the modern university with all its "faculties" (a sort of departmentalized brain) and its intellectual specialists, is untenable because of the **new nature of knowledge**.

Knowledge is a post-industrial force of production

What's new is the production of a completely new type of **knower**.

"The old principle that the acquisition of knowledge is indissociable from the **training** of minds ... is becoming obsolete and will become ever more so. The relationship of the suppliers and users of knowledge to the knowledge they supply and use is now tending ... to assume the form already taken by the relationship of commodity producers and consumers to the commodities they produce and consume - that is, the **form of value**. Knowledge is and will be produced in order to be sold, it is and will be consumed in order to be valorized in a new production: in both cases, the goal is exchange. Knowledge ceases to be an end in itself, it loses its 'use-value'".

The irreversible change from **knower** to **consumer of knowledge** is the cornerstone of postmodernity. This is the real historic change which legitimizes postmodernism - and not, as is usually claimed, the "change" to postmodern architecture.

Postmodernism which took shape in the 1970s might just have remained a European academic fad, except for two other successive developments which gave it real substance.

1. Science
-the new information technology and its aim - **global cyberspace**
-the new cosmology and its aim - **The Theory of Everything**
-the new progress in genetics and its aim - the **Human Genome Project**

2. Politics
-the popularity of **neo-conservatism** and rise of the Respectable Right in the 1970s
-the collapse of the Berlin Wall symbolizing the complete triumph of a **free market economy** over a socialist command economy.

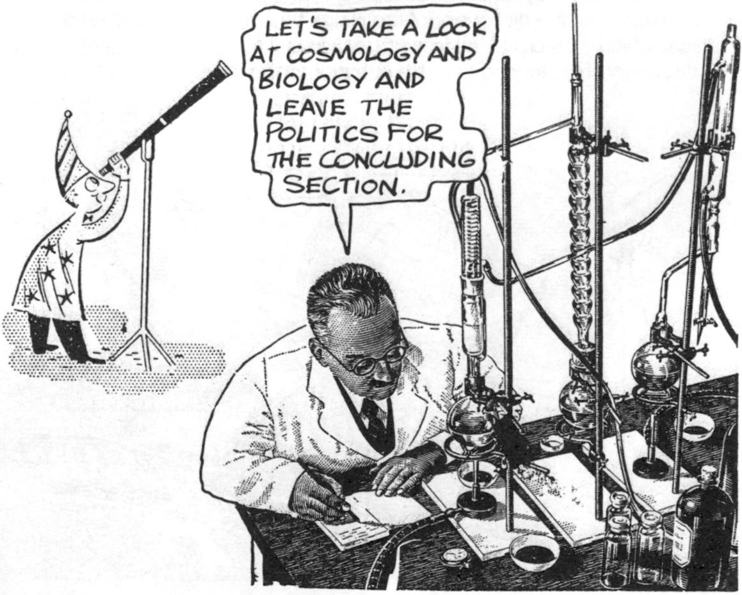

Theories of Everything

Stephen Hawking has encapsulated a theory of the entire universe in the famous last lines of his **Brief History of Time** (1987):

"...if we discover a complete theory, it should in time be understandable in broad principle by everyone... it would be the ultimate triumph of human reason - for then we will know the mind of God." As science gets closer and closer to this goal, it assumes postmodern relativist proportions. Relativism was introduced into science by Quantum mechanics. W.F.Heisenberg (1901-76) introduced a measure of permanent uncertainty in science with his principle: the impossibility of predicting both the mass and velocity of a particle at any given moment.

The "elementary" particle has turned out to be more and more elusive as we discover that the atom not only consists of protons, neutrons and electrons, but all varieties of gluons, charms, quarks... in a seemingly infinite count. Elementary entities in nature are now regarded by some as **strings** rather than **points.** Many scientists see string theory, which has solved the problems of space-time and internal symmetries, as a way forward towards a theory of everything. Hope is also pinned on the discovery of the Higgs boson, the so-called God particle, which is crucial to the understanding of the structure of matter - the discovery could lead to a single equation of the universe.

New developments in mathematics, however, suggest that there are serious limits to our scientific knowledge. The emerging theories of chaos and complexity demolish the notion of control and certainty in science. Chaos can be defined as a kind of order without periodicity. Complexity is concerned with complex systems in which a host of independent agents act with each other to produce spontaneous self-organisation. Both theories promise a postmodern revolution in science based on notions of holism, interconnection and order out of chaos and the idea of an autonomous, self-governing nature. Complexity grapples with big questions: what is life, why is there something rather than nothing, why do stock markets crash, why do ancient species remain stable in fossil records over millions of years, etc. While both chaos and complexity have forced us to ask sensible questions and to stop making naive assumptions, both are presented by their champions as new theories of everything. Complexity, for example, is championed as "**the** theory which includes the entire spectrum, from embryological development, evolution, the dynamics of ecosystems, complex societies, right up to Gaia: it's a theory of everything!"

Such totalizing tendencies in science have come under attack. Critiques of science from several disciplines (sociology, philosophy, anthropology and history) have attacked science for its notion of truth and rationality as well as the alleged objectivity of scientific method. All this criticism has established that science is a social process, that scientific method is little short of a myth, that scientific knowledge is in fact manufactured.

Postmodern science can be said to be in a condition of **anarchy**, a position affirmed as a good thing by the self-styled Dadaist philosopher of science, Paul Feyerabend.

"The only principle that does not inhibit progress is: anything goes...Without chaos, no knowledge. Without a frequent dismissal of reason, no progress...For what appears as 'sloppiness', 'chaos', or 'opportunism'...has a most important function in the development of those very theories which we today regard as essential parts of our knowledge ...These 'deviations', these 'errors', are preconditions of progress."

Against Method, 1988

The Anthropic Principle

We have seen how postmodern theories tend to belittle the human subject as a fictitious "construct". Postmodern cosmology has put the human being back into the picture, indeed in the very forefront of the universe, with its **anthropic principle**.
The principle states that human life has evolved in the way it has because the universe is of a certain size and a certain age.

At its strongest, the anthropic principle suggests that human consciousness is somehow "fitted" to the universe, not only as a component but as an **observation** necessary to give the universe meaning.
Quantum physicist Niels Bohr (1885-1962) proposed that no phenomenon can be said to exist unless it is an **observed** phenomenon.

A Retraction...

On page 16 we suggested that Cubism and modern Einsteinian physics shared in a discovery, a parallel way of seeing reality. This is a cliché accepted by some art historians. It is **false**!

Cubism's simplification of space and figures to geometric shapes has nothing whatsoever to do with Einstein's laws of relativity which describe a universe of curved space and warped time. Art and science totally part company at this point.

Art after Cubism continued down a road that was classically Newtonian, only to arrive at a visual dead end in the so-called Op or Kinetic art and minimalism of the 1960s. An outmoded fundamentalist faith in the classical purity of geometry can best be seen in the work of Victor Vasarely (b.1908), trained in the Hungarian branch of the Bauhaus.

HMM... LOOKS JUST LIKE ONE OF MY PAINTINGS!

We allowed the cliché to pass so that its incorrectness might better show up in the light of postmodern theory and science.

Genetics

Genetics is the study of genes, the basic constituents of all living matter. Genes, made of DNA molecules, are our driving force. It is through our genes that we reproduce and propagate ourselves. Some geneticists claim that natural selection over thousands of generations has programmed human behaviour and emotional responses in our genes. Scientists are trying to identify genes that influence behaviour in the hope that we will understand what we are and who we are, when we know what our genes are made of.

Genetics has been used for decades to engineer crops to resist viral diseases and insects, produce better vegetables and fruits and improve breeds of cattle. Increasingly, it is being used in medicine to fight genetically inherited diseases. Now, the **Human Genome Project**, a multi-billion dollar research endeavour extending over several decades, aims to map out and analyze the complete genetic blueprint for a human being. A gene is a long sequence of four kinds of nucleotides identified by the letters A,T,C and G. The project aims to write down the nucleotide sequence A's,T's, C's and G's of all the genes of human beings. The knowledge will be extremely useful in treating and curing some genetically caused diseases, like cystic fibrosis and thalassaemia

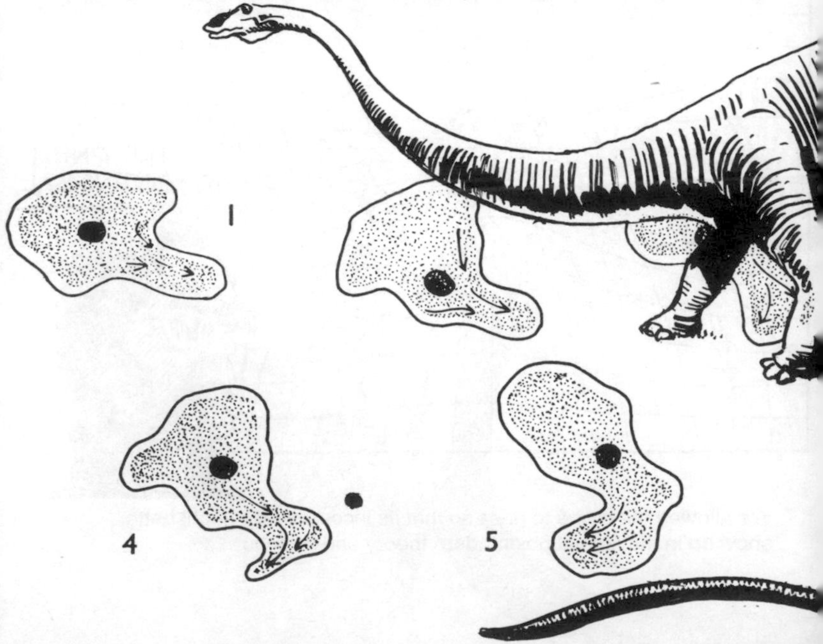

or sickle-cell anaemia. But more than that - the Human Genome Project, it has been claimed, is an attempt to find out how to spell "human". It will thus transform the very concept of human nature and mark the culmination of the scientific revolution begun by Darwin.

At the very least, the Human Genome Project will have direct consequences for those seeking medical care, family planning, investors seeking to save for pensions, insurance companies trying to assess actuarial risks, and for prospective employers assessing the health and capabilities of their workers.

Critics of the Human Genome Project argue that the reduction of the human being to no more than the biological expression of the programme of instructions encoded in his or her DNA will have serious moral consequences on how we look at ourselves.

Determinists are in danger of hunting for the "Cinderella" gene - those particular genes which in isolation pre-determine just about everything from intelligence to homosexuality, free market entrepreneurs and male dominance. If we accept that innate differences and abilities are written in our genes and biologically inherited, then hierarchy is actually encoded in human nature. The world is the way it is because that is exactly how it should be. A proposed scientific explanation thus becomes the instrument for legitimizing the **status quo**.

PART THREE: THE GENEALOGY OF POSTMODERN HISTORY

Can we speak of a postmodern "history"? Not if we take postmodern theory seriously, which challenges the very idea of a unilinear history. Postmodernism cannot follow in sequence after modernism, because this would be an admission of historic progress and a relapse into Grand Narrative mythology.

Architecture claims to have a precise date for the inauguration of postmodernism...

3:32 p.m. on 15 July 1972...

the Pruitt-Igoe housing development in St. Louis, Missouri, a prize-winning complex designed for low income people, was dynamited as uninhabitable.

According to Charles Jencks, this proclaimed the death of the International Style of modernist architecture, the end of buildings as "machines for living" envisioned for us by Mies van der Rohe, Gropius, Le Corbusier and other abstract functionalists.

Po Mo Vernacular

Also in 1972, the American architect Robert Venturi (b.1925) formulated the postmodern creed.

In place of unilateral "glass boxes", po mo architecture offers the **vernacular**, an emphasis on the local and particular as opposed to modernist universalism. This means a return to ornament, with references to the historic past and its symbolism, but in the ironic manner of parody, pastiche and **quotation**.

Venturi and other postmoderns propose a "comicstrip" architecture - eclectic, ambiguous, humorous. Unpretentious, in short.

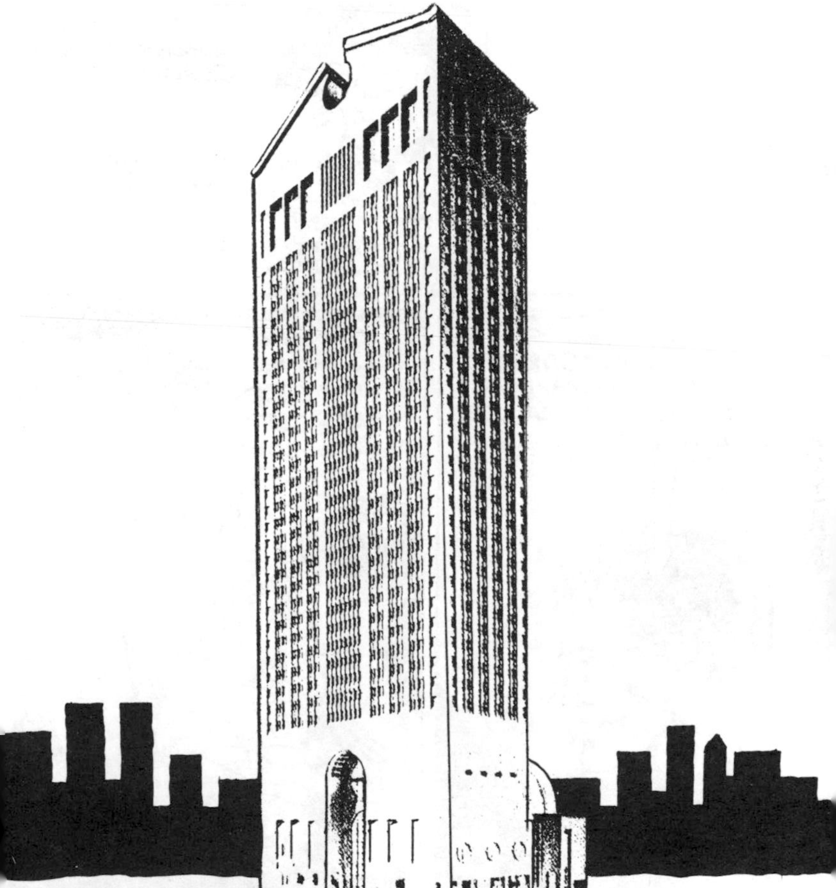

An example of this is Philip Johnson (a defector from High Modernism) who produced the New York A.T.&T. Building in the shape of a grandfather clock topped off with a Chippendale broken pediment.

Po mo architecture's ironic energy, its radical eclecticism, seem to give immediate credibility to postmodern theory. This is because the building itself serves as visible proof of the theory.

High modernist visionaries like Le Corbusier believed they could achieve the transformation of social life by transforming architectural space as a substitute for **political** revolution.

Computerizing Difference

Modernist experimenters failed to change the world of capitalism - in fact, the utopian purity of their glass towers ended by glorifying the power of banks, airlines and multinational corporations.

COMPUTER-MODELLING, AUTOMATED PRODUCTION AND SOPHISTICATED MARKET RESEARCH NOW ALLOW US TO MASS-PRODUCE A VARIETY OF STYLES AND ALMOST PERSONALIZED PRODUCTS.
BEEP!

Similarly, po mo architects cannot avoid being employees of late capitalism. They cannot invent a "history" simply by changing the look of buildings. Besides which, po mo architecture continues to use the construction materials and the mass production techniques of modernism - but with an added novelty - **the computer**. Theorists like Charles Jencks believe the computer can replace the stereotyped uniformity of modernism by **multiplying difference...**

Simulated Reality and Disneyland

Pluralism, "multiplying difference", is the brave new hope of postmodernism. Trying to achieve it by computer or **electronic simulation** is an illusion.

Venturi's choice of Disneyland as a model of the postmodern is equally in trouble. Disneyland is entirely simulated, a scrubbed-clean replica of Main Street U.S.A. electronically annexed to theme park hyperreality. It is the utopian version of Bladerunner's dystopian Los Angeles where replicants run amok.
METRO

You see nothing of Disneyland reproduced on these pages because it is a totalitarian corporation paranoiac in defence of its copyright. 100% pure simulated reproduction prohibits reproduction! But you can see Disneyland as a reflection of blissful contentment on the faces of its visitors.

Welcome to the Holocaust Theme Park

ARBEIT MACHT FREI

Another sort of Disneyland hyperreal tour of the past is offered at the Holocaust Memorial Museum in Washington DC - a "theme park" stroll through genocide.

On admission you are issued with an ID card, matching your age and gender to the name and photo of a real Holocaust victim or survivor. As you progress through 3 floors of the exhibition, you can push your bar-coded card into computer stations and see how well or badly your real life subject is faring. Will you (like him or her) end up saved, shot, gassed, incinerated? You'll find extermination camp bunks on which inmates lay unspeakably crammed, dying of malnutrition and typhus. You'll see the ovens in which victims of Zyklon-B gassings were burnt.

Worst of all is the endlessly re-run video footage of **Einsatzgruppen** mass-killing squads at work, shooting, stabbing, filling ditches with piles of naked corpses. You are watching **historical snuff movies**.

Have you really experienced the Holocaust in this postmodern theme park? At the end, you'll find visitors' ID cards dumped in litter bins among the pop bottles and chocolate wrappers. Your hyper-reality tour is over.

WHAT YOU SEE IS WHAT YOU GET

The Installation of Memory Loss

To apply the museum techniques of installation art to the Holocaust must render it a timeless object of aesthetic viewing - a **postmodern readymade**.

The Holocaust will remain a death mask effigy of modernity to which we will address the insoluble question: Is this where modern rationalism leads, to mass-industrialized killing?

Forgetfulness at the gates of Auschwitz...and beyond to its past in the future...

"even the most extreme consciousness of doom threatens to degenerate into idle chatter. Cultural criticism finds itself faced with the final stage of the dialectic of culture and barbarism. ***To write poetry after Auschwitz is barbaric.*** And this corrodes even the knowledge of ***why*** it has become impossible to write poetry today. Absolute reification, which presupposed intellectual progress as one of its elements, is now preparing to absorb the mind entirely. Critical intelligence cannot be equal to this challenge as long as it confines itself to self-satisfied contemplation."

T.W.Adorno, **Prisms**,1956

The opposite of knowledge is not ignorance but deceit and fraud.

Hypermodernism: the Memory Loss of Reality

We are entering (have entered?) an amnesiac zone of "postmodernity" which should be called **hypermodernism**. The meaning of so-called postmodernism turns out to be a technological hyper-intensification of modernism. Technology and economics merge and are disguised by alternative labels - **post-industrial, electronic, services, information, computer economy** - each of which contributes to hyperreal processing and simulation. An example: **olestra**, a sucrose polyester of hyperreal fat.

OLESTRA
OLESTRA TASTES LIKE FAT, ACTS LIKE FAT IN COOKING AND WILL STAIN YOUR TIE IF YOU DROP SOME ON IT...
...BUT IT'S IN NO SENSE A FOOD BECAUSE YOUR DIGESTIVE ENZYMES CAN'T GET A GRIP ON IT. IT'S DIGESTIVELY INERT.
UNLIKE THIS.

Hyperreal Finance

Here's a far more spectacular example of "digestive inertness". The world financial markets are hooked-up for 24-hour non-stop trading. In this imaginary space of cellular phones, modems, computers and faxes, a Wall Street firm of takeover specialists can swiftly raid and strip a giant corporation. Hundreds of millions of dollars slosh around...

What happens to the corporation that took years to build up? Does it matter **what** it produced? It has no more relevance to financial hyperreality than sucrose polyester on the digestion.

Welcome to Cyberia!

The term **cyberspace** was coined by science-fiction writer William Gibson in his novel **Neuromancer** and defined as "consensual hallucination". The term came to be applied to the "room" or any space generated by software within a computer that produces a Virtual-Reality (VR) experience. VR is a computer-mediated, multisensory experience, one designed to trick our senses and convince us that we are "in another world". In VR world, the computer takes complete control and guides the way of sensing, feeling and thinking of the participants. More generally, cyberspace is the "nowhere space" in the telephone line between you and where all things on-line happen. The artificial landscape on Internet or Compuserve, computer networks that connect millions of users throughout the world, through which one can move, download information, talk to other users, visit special discussion forums, shop, make airline and hotel bookings, is cyberspace.

Cyber is one of the most used prefixes of the 90s, signifying a world of computer dominance and disembodied experience. All those seeking computer driven transcendence and travel through cyberspace are **cybernauts**. The word that actually started all the cyber-enthusiasm, **cyberpunk**, began as a subgenre of science fiction popular in the late 80s. Cyberpunk represents the implosion of the future into the present and total intrusion of technology into human lives. Here giant corporations wield more power than governments, anarchistic computer hackers lead rebellions against them on the new frontier of global networks, the human body goes cyborg, augmented by chemicals, bionic prosthetics and neural implants. The culture spawned by cyberpunks and cybernauts is - what else? - **cyberculture**. The civilization springing up on-line is **Cyberia**.

A Walk on the Wild Side

The true neuromancer-theorist of po mo Cyberia is Jean Baudrillard (who introduced the 4 phases of the image on page 55). Let's walk with Baudrillard into Virtual Reality.

Step 1. The image is a reflection of a basic reality.

A painting by Van Gogh. A pair of rough peasant shoes, nothing else. Actually the painting represents nothing. But as to what ***is*** *in that picture, you are immediately alone with it as though you yourself were making your way wearily homeward with your hoe on an evening in late autumn after the last potato fires have died down...*

Martin Heidegger, from **The Origin of the Work of Art**

Step 2. The image masks and perverts a basic reality.

Step 3. The image marks the absence of a basic reality.

Fashionable? That depends on your definition. But we hear that they're even wearing Timberlands on the Champs Elysées these days. For more information about our rugged Timberland gear, ring us free on 0800 320 500.
Timberland
BOOTS, SHOES, CLOTHING,

Now we pass to the modern industrial age of **mass reproduction.**

Step 4. The postmodern simulacrum

A pair of trainers...they are simulacra, expensive street-cred models, sportswear with nothing to do with sport. The slogan advertising Nike Air Jordans goes like this: "Get some get some get some get some."

You can be mugged or killed for desirable sportswear. Detroit, 1985, Shawn Jones, 13, shot for his Fila sneakers. Houston, 1988, fatal stabbing over a pair of tennis shoes. Detroit, 1989 and Philadelphia 1990, two schoolboys murdered for their sneakers...get some get some get some...

The War as NOT seen on TV

On the eve of the Gulf War (16 January to 28 February 1991), Baudrillard famously remarked that there **couldn't** be a war. Why not? Because "War itself has entered a definitive crisis. It is too late for a 'hot' Third World War. The moment has passed. It has been distilled in the course of time into the Cold War and there will be no other...The reciprocal deterrent between the two blocs (USA vs. USSR) worked because of what might be termed the excess means of destruction. Today it works even better as a total self-deterrent, which has gone so far as to create the self-dissolution of the Eastern bloc..."

Liberation,11/1/91

The first Cyberwar?

After the war, Baudrillard still argued that it had not occurred. It was only a hyperreal representation on our TV screens.

The battlefield realities of the past had been replaced by mass media saturation coverage with its talk of "smart bombs" and "collateral damage". Military strategists, politicians, commentators, newspaper readers and TV viewers were all channelled into a vast disinformation simulator which programmed what they thought, saw and did.
"...It was as if the outcome had been devoured in advance by a parasitic virus, the retro-virus of history. This is why one could offer the hypothesis that this war would not have taken place. And now that it is over, one can finally take account of its non-occurrence."

Since then, have we not been media hostages witnessing other wars which also did not happen? The interminable decimation of Bosnia in former Yugoslavia? The genocide of Tutsi by Hutu in Rwanda? "...a form of war," as Baudrillard says, "which means never needing to face up to war, which enables war to be 'perceived' from deep within a darkroom."

YES, **HYPER-SCEPTICISM**. INTELLECTUALS MUST STOP LEGITIMIZING THE NOTION THAT THERE IS SOME "ULTIMATE TRUTH" BEHIND APPEARANCES. THEN, MAYBE, THE MASSES WILL TURN THEIR BACKS ON THE MEDIA AND PUBLIC OPINION MANAGEMENT WILL COLLAPSE.
CNN
LIVE
CNN
LIVE

Baudrillard has been criticized for extreme nihilism. Does he offer any hope to the "masses" (what he calls the captive TV and mass media consumers)?

Only (re)Produce

The opposite of knowledge is not ignorance but deceit and fraud.

Baudrillard's notional scepticism is unconvincing. But his exaggerated views on media cyberpower highlights a condition that needs urgent emphasizing.

The last 25 years of the 20th century will go down in history as unique in one respect. These "postmodern" years are symptomatic of a total lack of originality. Our scanty resources of invention are all parasitically confined to **reproduction**. Everything apparently "new" - whether it be CDs, cyberspace Virtual Reality or even the DNA Genome Project and postmodern cosmology - is feeding on the originality of the past, on a data bank not simply of information but of **already experienced** reality.

Why have we come to this unprecedented technologically-streamlined **cannibalization**? Could it be that we are commanded by an unconscious, biologically determined will (a "selfish gene") to proceed with the absolute demolition of the past for a reason that we cannot comprehend? Are we "wiping the slate clean" for the coming of the artificially engineered human?

This is a paranoiac vision of reproduction, a sci-fi pessimistic advent of the **in**human.
We might do better to reconsider Marx's view of capitalist reproduction. The reality of capitalist production is that of a process which unfolds in time, one cycle of production succeeded by another: a question of **continuity** in short, which is a problem of social and economic **re**production.

For capitalist production to be continuous in time, it must not only reproduce itself completely but **expand** the fundamental conditions of its mode of production. The question arises: How can this continuity of production be maintained, when the value and global extent of this production seem to result from individual decisions by thousands of businessmen who **hide their intentions from each other**?

The players of the capitalist game must inevitably be "in deceit", and a sort of acceptable consensus of fraud must be basic to the continuous reproductive expansion of its mode of production.

And this is why everything "postmodern" so nakedly depends on and stems from reproduction. The game is about fabricating a sort of knowledge, which although it **looks** to be expanding and becoming accessible to a vast public on the internet superhighways, is in fact becoming industrially controlled.

So, when Lyotard replaces the traditionally-trained knower with the "knower as consumer", he is not valorizing either the "new" knower or the novelties of knowledge, but is implicitly acknowledging the omnipotence of the free market economy.

The new-born consumer of knowledge enters with amnesia into an already established game of deceit. He, she, is a myth of postmodernity.

Now let's continue our walk on the wild side, in search of this mythical "knower as consumer" in his or her postmodern habitat, the **Cyberian streetscenes**...

Advertising Hyperreality

The object of advertising now is not merely to create dreams and desires, but to engender a new commodified reality shaped by a company's logo or slogan. The notorious Benetton ads provide a good example of how advertising has embraced postmodernism. The campaign consists of bold photographs - a white woman and a black woman holding an oriental baby wrapped in a towel, the breasts of a black woman being sucked by a white baby, a child's black hand resting on a white male hand - accompanied with the company logo: **United Colors of Benetton**.

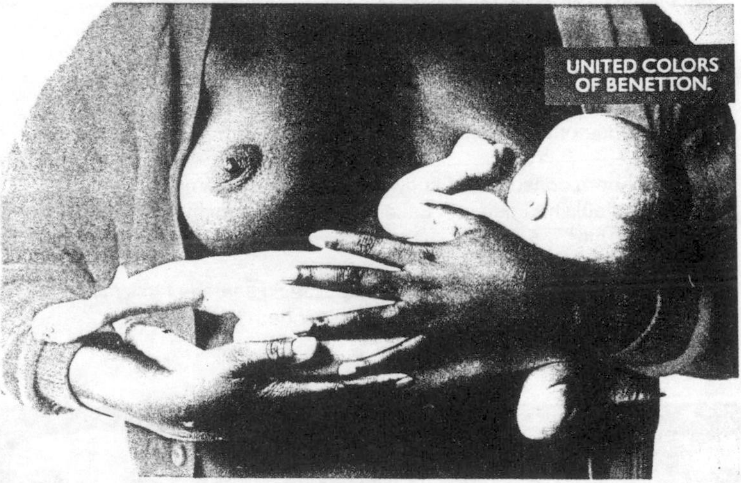

The photographs themselves do not convey any message about buying brightly coloured knitwear, but the slogan connotes a reference to the company's image - an international brand name of global identity and distinction.

Benetton appropriates and transforms photo-journalism into advertising to undermine the cultural codes by which advertising images are seen as unreal, as well as to commodify the hyperreality of the news photo and cash in on the news value of the images. Benetton advertisements have carried news photographs of a dying AIDS patient with his distraught family, a picture of a graveyard with rows of white crosses after the Gulf War and of an African mercenary holding a human thigh bone.

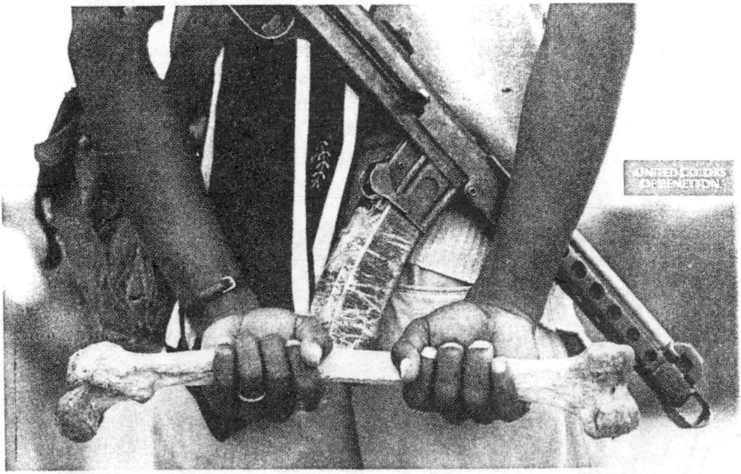

The African mercenary is an iconic image: deprived of history and context, it excavates all that represents the Africans as barbaric flesh-eaters incapable of embracing civilization. The image refers to a moment of barbarism, having no reference to the chain of events which led to it, while depriving the African of a voice. The Benetton campaign encapsulates the past, present and future in a single time frame offering images which conjure historic, futuristic and apocalyptic elements within a grammar of race. Difference is commodified and a portrait of plurality is produced which sets the colourful individuals within the image as a race apart. This is advertising as a "social conscience", an artificially constructed reality that projects an image of harmony to sell a brand name, while reproducing the stereotypes of Western culture.

"I wannabe a wigger"

A mutation of hip-hop and rap styles, **gangsta rap** started in the early 80s and became the dominant form of the genre. Using the buzz words of the street - nigger, bitch, ho (whore), icing cops - gangsta rappers celebrate violence towards women, the police and sadism, chauvinism, gang feuds, drug deals, sexual and black-on-black violence. What makes gangsta rap truly postmodern is that the gangsta rappers walk their talk: the violent images of the songs are reflected in the life of the rappers themselves. Rapper Snoop Doggy Dogg, whose album **Doggystyle** broke all records by going straight to number one slot and sold 3.5 million copies, has been indicted for murder. Rapper-actor, Tupac Shakur, was arrested for shooting two off-duty policemen in Atlanta. Flavor Flav of the group "Public Enemy" was arrested for allegedly trying to shoot a neighbour in New York...

While gangsta rappers sing of dispossessed ghetto-dwellers, most of their fans and listeners are in fact white suburban adolescents looking for a cause and style that gives them a sense of identity - those known in the vernacular as "wiggers", wannabe white niggers. Many blacks themselves have strongly condemned gangsta rap as racist and demeaning to blacks.

Karaoke...

Originally a masochistic playtime for stressed-out Japanese businessmen, **karaoke** has become a pandemic "vox pox" participatory performance art.

It is just a coincidence, of course, that karaoke developed after Japanese multinationals bought up leading recording companies and their backlists.

...and Serial Killings

...rivalling karaoke as the most popular copycat form of po mo performance art worldwide in films, TV and real life.

Typically, the film of the book **Silence of the Lambs** (1992) presented a cannibal psychopath as a genial, cultured, charismatic genius who alone is able to direct the hunt for another serial killer. It was one of only three films in Oscar history to take all five top awards.

Serial killers have always been with us, but the question is, why do they now have such a dominant hold on the popular imagination? Is it because they're the top dollar-earners of chequebook journalism, TV serialization and film? Because they represent value for money in promoting the "hyperreal" spectacle of evil, perversion and bloodlust?

X-rated Cybersex Games

On-line pornography can be downloaded from bulletin boards and global networks. You can interact with Lulu, the first porn star of Virtual Reality or play "Cyborgasm", a CD-ROM, whose three-dimensional effects would convince any user that he/she is participating in a no-holes-barred sexual encounter. Computer games are now available with an "X-rated" button; hit the gore button and you can celebrate your triumph by ripping out the head of your victim with the spinal cord dangling from it.

Cybersex fiction takes a quantum leap towards reality with the arrival of the "teledildonic" suit. This consists of a head-piece with video and audio input connected to a suit that stimulates the erogenous zones.

Players take on the idealized persona of the beautiful and sexually talented and enjoy a solitary on-line experience with pre-recorded programmes or interact with other networking participants. Distant, safe, uncommitted and uninvolved, Cybersex is the ultimate tonic for panic-ridden angst.

Cyborgs and Schwarzenegger

Detroit in the future: a bleak urban landscape dominated by anarchy and crime. A badly injured cop is reconstructed by science: part human, part machine, he takes on the forces of evil. **Robocop** (1987) was one of the new breed of postmodern films that magnify a playful mixing of images and reality, a dislocation and erasure of personal history and identity.

In David Lynch's **Blue Velvet** (1986), the central character moves between two incompatible worlds: on the one side, the adolescent world of small town USA in the 1950s with its high school and drugstore culture; and a bizarre, violent, sex-crazed world of drugs, dementia and sexual perversions on the other.
The protagonist is not sure which is true reality. Lynch's cult TV series **Twin Peaks** (1989) also blurs the frontier between hallucination and reality in a world shaped by dreams.

The icon of postmodern cinema is Arnold Schwarzenegger. His muscle-bound physique, lack of emotion, total absence of sweat and inability to act serve as an ideal blank on which to over-write coded messages of considerable postmodern sophistication.
In **Terminator** (1984) he is a cyborg sent from the future to change the

present, while the film itself retells the New Testament in the genre of science fiction. In **Total Recall** (1990) he is a secret agent with a missing memory and confused identity. He fights three worlds - Earth, Mars and the evil Recall corporation - which have colluded to erase his personal history and change his identity. In **The Last Action Hero** (1993) we are presented with three Schwarzeneggers: one acting in the film before us, one in the film within the film and the "real" one who happens to be attending the première of his film, with his real wife, in the film.

Madonna, Cybergirl

Postmodern icon of the 80s, stringy-muscled frame and identikit face - who is she?
Madonna has been appropriately dubbed "the Queen of Appropriation", taking on the personae of Hollywood superstars and even presenting herself as an all-purpose porn sex object.
She has gone through a Marilyn Monroe period, a pastiche of 70s images in the **Deeper and Deeper** video, the dizzying incarnation of classic stars from Lauren Bacall to Marlene Dietrich for the **Vogue** video, and recreated herself as a sadomasochist alley cat for her book **Sex**. What does it all add up to? For some, Madonna is the cyber-model of the New Woman.

Comicbook superheroes like Batman have the habit of wearing their underpants over their tights. Super-Madonna wears a corset over her street-clothes.

Madonna specializes in the very thing that so many feminists have condemned in advertising - the dismembered "part object" fetishism of the female body.

FASHION'S most romantic story for seasons has been the rise of the corset. Dolce and Gabbana and Christian Lacroix both caught up with Vivienne Westwood and John Galliano who have long been devotees of the garment, now sexy, which used to symbolise figure fascism.

Women are begging to wear them, although the work that goes into the boning makes them very expensive. Rigby and Peller, the queen's corsetier, tailors similar corsets or basques from £550. Alternatively there's the real McCoy which tend to be much cheaper. Cornucopia has an ever-changing selection of Victorian corsets and tops from boned dresses which have been long separated from their skirts. Worn over a simple slip skirt they are the alternative to bias cutting for evening.

Find Rigby and Peller at 2 Hans Road, SW3, and Cornucopia at 12 Upper Tachbrook Street, SW1.

Tamasin Doe

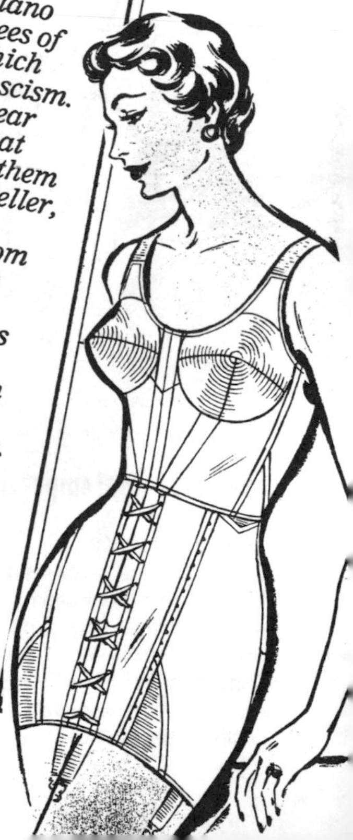

Evening Standard, 12 July 1994.

Zapping or Zero-Consciousness

Create your own TV collage of life by switching from news to soap-opera to sport to documentary to feature film, to the hi-fi system to a quick burst of karaoke. Zapping was born with the arrival of multi-channel cable and satellite broadcasting, coupled with the indispensable aid of the hand-held remote control. This seeming cornucopia of choice to cater to the diversity of individual interest ends up with everyone choosing to watch nothing - the art is in zapping, the auto-creation of your very own postmodern spectacle.

Endlessly Contemporary Amnesia

1. Hyperactivity

Zapping - or zero-consciousness - is a postmodern symptom of impatience without depth. The traditional richness and subtlety of nature, art and religion have faded away before our eyes and we are left with a "recession of reality".

Zapped-out zero-consciousness is also a product of "post-industrial" hyperactivity and extreme anxiety posed by high unemployment and its Japanese-style alternative, "management by stress".

2. Zapping out the past...

The media have substituted themselves for the older world. Even if we should wish to recover that older world we can do it only by an intensive study of the ways in which the media have swallowed it.

Marshall McLuhan

The destruction of the past is one of the most characteristic and eerie phenomena of the late 20th century. Most young men and women at the century's end grow up in a sort of permanent present lacking any organic relation to the public past of the times they live in.

Eric Hobsbawm, **Age of Extremes: the Short Twentieth Century 1914-1991**

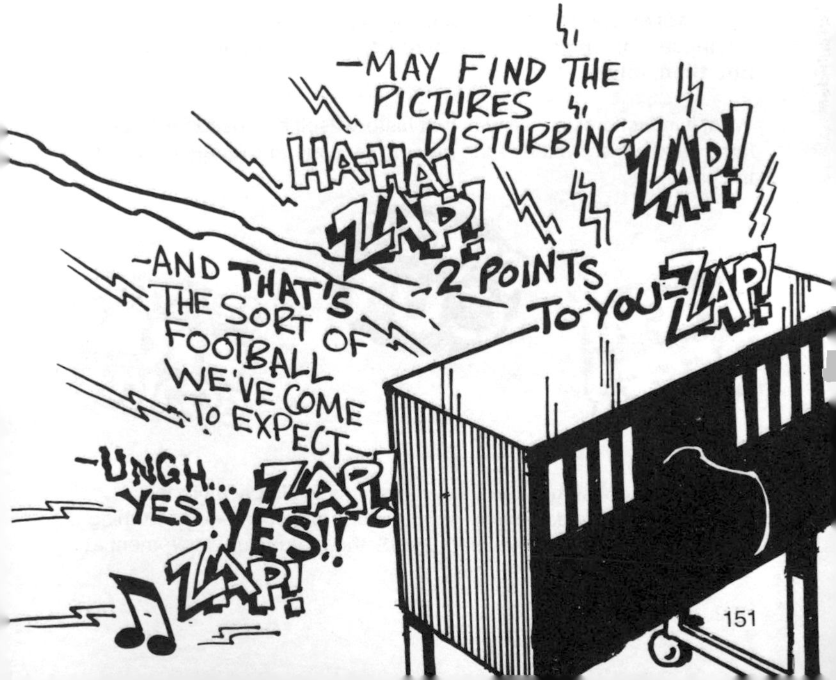

Zapped-out Hypermodernism

Like so much else in our world, postmodernity's amnesiac zero-consciousness proceeds from modernism.

"Modern" was a problem name from the start. It is unsatisfactory in a way different from other earlier period names, such as Renaissance, Baroque, Romantic, etc. Modern is a highly volatile term. There is a sell-by-date obsolescence built into it, an insistence on renewable originality, a sort of constantly renovated virtuosity that tires very quickly. "Modern" is at best a category of fashion, not a term which can give any assurance of stability.

Modern is a **panic** term. It swept into history with a sense that a catastrophic change had overtaken tradition. Modern**ism** was defined by a set of innovative artistic practices which became confused with the much wider cultural and historical implications of **modernity**. Avantgarde artists seemed to be the gauge registering the shock waves of something catastrophic in history, a **present time** of high-speed stimulation **without forseeable end.**

Modernist art claimed to be producing works independent of all reference, not representational of reality but **pure signs of nothing but themselves**.

What it in fact proclaimed was that history itself had become plugged into consumerist hysteria - the present as a mega clearance sale of the past.

Postmodern consumer zero-consciousness is simply a higher degree of hypermodernism in which all of production seems nothing but a pure sign of itself. Acceleration **IS** the status quo. Movement at a standstill...

Icons of the Respectable Right

"Movement at a standstill" finds its mirror-likeness in an equally paradoxical formulation, **radical conservatism**. Warhol, Madonna, Schwarzenegger and such like are not the true icons of postmodernity which is more intriguingly represented by Pope John Paul II, Maggie Thatcher and Ronald Reagan. All three have interpreted postmodernity as a shift, not a change, in the power structure that is supported by the wide-based popularity of conservatism.

Pope John Paul (Karol Wojtyla) came along in 1978 to put an end to the liberal reforms of the Catholic Church begun by Pope John XXIII (1958-63).

Similarly, liberalism and social democracy went into reverse course with the arrival of President Reagan (1981) and Prime Minister Thatcher (1979).

What these leaders and other New Right postmoderns foresaw was the ending of the Cold War by the worldwide success of a freemarket economy.

OF COURSE THE FREE MARKET MUST TRIUMPH OVER COMMUNISM. AS AN EAST EUROPEAN, I KNOW IT!
AH - MUSIC TO MY EARS!
DO TELL US MORE, YOUR HOLINESS...

COMMUNISTS HAVE TOTALLY MISUNDERSTOOD MODERN TECHNOLOGY. IT'S RUN FOR PARTY BOSSES AND NOT DESIGNED TO DELIVER TO THE CONSUMER. SOONER OR LATER, THE HUNGER FOR COMMODITIES WILL DRIVE THE MASSES TO DEMAND THEIR FRANCHISE IN TECHNOLOGY — THEIR RIGHT TO A PROSPERITY THAT DOESN'T REALLY EXIST!

SUPPOSE THE COMMIES ARE SMART ENOUGH TO INTRODUCE MARKET REFORMS?
THAT'S EXACTLY WHAT GORBACHEV TRIED TO DO IN THE LATE 80s. RESULT? THE SOVIET UNION FELL APART LIKE HUMPTY DUMPTY!
WOULD POSTMODERNISM BE SUCH A POWERFUL IDEA IF COMMUNISM HADN'T DISINTEGRATED?
BY THE WAY, YOUR HOLINESS, HAVE YOU EVER THOUGHT OF EXCOMMUNICATING **MADONNA**?
HMM YES... I BELIEVE THE AYATOLLAH KHOMEINI HAS TRIED SOMETHING LIKE THAT WITH A PESKY WRITER...

The Satanic Verses and Postmodern Panic

On 14 February 1989, Iran's leader the Ayatollah Khomeini issued his **fatwa** which sentenced to death Salman Rushdie, a British writer born in India, for apostasy and blasphemy against the faith of Islam. Rushdie's novel, **The Satanic Verses**, had provoked the **fatwa** and the anger of Muslims throughout the world.

Why such a deadly fuss over a work of fiction? The issue for the Ayatollah wasn't merely that of a novel...

Khomeini's **fatwa** was an astute political manoeuvre in the aftermath of the **first** Gulf War which began with Iraq's invasion of Iran in 1980 and dragged on inconclusively till 1988. Western powers sided with Iraq's dictator Saddam Hussein against Iran's fundamentalist regime. Khomeini's **fatwa** was partly a reprisal for this Western opposition. Three years later, Saddam Hussein used the arms supplied by the West against the West in the **second** Gulf War.

The Rushdie affair is a war of non-communication between two entrenched "panic positions". Muslims object to Rushdie's blurring of boundaries between fiction and real history which for them enshrines the Prophet Muhammad's revelation. Westerners defend Rushdie's right to treat Islam as simply another postmodern "Grand Narrative".

Rushdie defended himself by appealing to historical enlightenment.

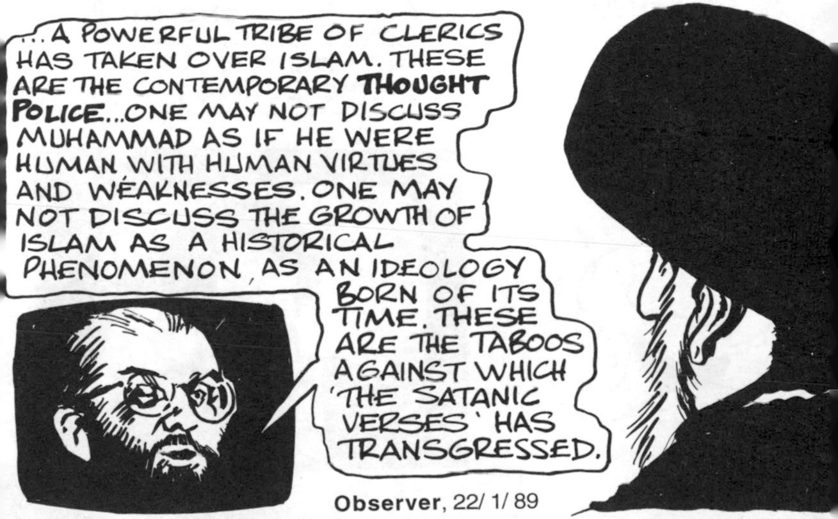
...A POWERFUL TRIBE OF CLERICS HAS TAKEN OVER ISLAM. THESE ARE THE CONTEMPORARY **THOUGHT POLICE**...ONE MAY NOT DISCUSS MUHAMMAD AS IF HE WERE HUMAN WITH HUMAN VIRTUES AND WEAKNESSES. ONE MAY NOT DISCUSS THE GROWTH OF ISLAM AS A HISTORICAL PHENOMENON, AS AN IDEOLOGY BORN OF ITS TIME. THESE ARE THE TABOOS AGAINST WHICH 'THE SATANIC VERSES' HAS TRANSGRESSED.

Observer, 22/ 1/ 89

On the day of the **fatwa**, Rushdie said in an interview...

DOUBT, IT SEEMS TO ME, IS THE CENTRAL CONDITION OF A HUMAN BEING IN THE 20TH CENTURY. ONE OF THE THINGS THAT HAS HAPPENED TO US... IS TO LEARN HOW **CERTAINTY** CRUMBLES IN YOUR HAND.

The question is, why should Muslims - or anyone else - embrace doubt as **their** central condition? Is it the **only** legitimate condition? And legitimized by whom? This too is a central postmodern question.

What of the **fatwa** itself? Is capital punishment for apostasy really legitimate in Islam?

APOSTATES HAVE EXISTED IN ISLAM BEFORE, SOME EVEN IN THE PROPHET'S OWN TIME, MANY OF THEM GREAT LITERARY FIGURES – BUT NONE OF THEM HAVE BEEN EXECUTED. THERE IS NO SANCTION FOR SUCH AN ACTION IN THE QURAN.

A **fatwa** is a juristic opinion, not law. It is only binding on the person who gives it and those who accept his **taqlid** (blind following). It has nothing to do with the position of the majority of Muslims who do not support state terrorism.

The question of "blind following" is not limited, however, to Iranian territory.

The West cannot see itself as an "arms dealer" exporting postmodern scepticism - a supplier of doubt against Islam's certainty, of secularism against sacredness, of sabotage against the Quran's revelation and a deconstruction of the Prophet's truth as one more relative notion.
This is the postmodern paradox - doubt which is itself in doubt and which ought therefore to be more tolerant of other's beliefs (but isn't, really).

So, if Rushdie is a typical postmodern writer, then the Ayatollah is a typical product of the postmodern assault on the sacred and its panicked defence. Fundamentalism - whether of the Muslim, Christian or Jewish sort - is the panic interface of postmodernism.

Third World Postmodernism

Islam and the so-called Third World are left out of most accounts of postmodernism. Foucault's teaching has not apparently succeeded to inspire much suspicion about why they are excluded from history.

What does postmodernism look like from a Third World perspective? Let's look at music for a start...

Quawwali is the devotional music of India, Pakistan and Bangladesh. Of Sufi origins, it is sung to the simple rhythm of traditional drums and hand-clapping in praise of God, Prophet Muhammad, Ali the fourth Caliph of Islam and classical Sufi masters. The postmodern revival of Quawwali owes a great deal to Martin Scorsese's film **The Last Temptation of Christ** where Quawwali and other Islamic music provided passionate musical backing to a narrative that, ironically, tried to undermine the religious sanctity of its subject matter.

But in the Subcontinent it has gone funky and is sung to a syncopated rock beat generated by synthesizers. What was originally designed to induce mystical ecstasy is now used to generate hysteria for rock music. Even more postmodern is the juxtaposition of Hindu fundamentalism in politics with trendy Hindu youths bopping to the beat of updated Sufi music!

Traditional non-Western music has become fair game for postmodern appropriation. Music from Zaire, the Solomon Islands, Burundi, the Sahel, Iran, Turkey and elsewhere is freely blended with New Age electronics and rock beats to make it palatable to Western tastes. African Pygmies go postmodern on "Deep Forest"!

Third World postmodernism parallels the condition of colonial or neo-colonial dependency on shop-worn and out-of-fashion goods, irrelevant or useless technology, expensive or banned drugs, exported to the developing countries where they enjoy a profitable second life. As with the frenzy of modernization in the 50s and 60s, post-modernism has been embraced uncritically and enthusiastically by some and resisted strongly by others. Modern Indian cinema and pop music, Malay hard rock and the work of postmodernist novelists like Thailand's Somtow celebrate postmodernism wholeheartedly. South African township jive music, contemporary Filipino film, the punk rock culture of Medellin cocaine slums in Colombia take a more critical stance towards postmodernism. Kenyan novelist Ngugi wa Thiongo's decision to abandon the novel and write mainly in Kikuyu and Rigoberta Menchu's striking testimonial narrative of Indian resistance in Guatemala, **I, Rigoberta Menchu**, have transformed postmodernism into a culture of resistance. Third World postmodernism is as diverse as Third World cultures themselves.

Nowhere in the Third World is postmodernism more contested than in Latin America. During the Reagan era, a postmodernism of the **right** flourished throughout Latin America. The 1990 rival presidential campaigns of novelist Mario Vargas Llosa and Alberto Fujimori in Peru, the media populism of Carlos Menem in Argentina (1989) and Fernando Collor in Brazil (1990), the transformation of Mexico in prospect of the North American Free Trade Agreement, and the complex politics and economics of drugs and terrorism are the high points of rightwing postmodernism.
These developments led the Mexican poet and Nobel Laureate, Octavio Paz, to describe postmodernism as yet another imported project that does not fit Latin America. The South American left, on the other hand, sees the postmodern project as an important means of renovating its exhausted and discredited political agenda. A " left postmodernism", based on the "ethos of survival", has emerged to challenge the gains of the right.

Perhaps the most noted champions of this variety of Latin American postmodernism are the Sandinistas of Nicaragua who, after their defeat, embraced a whole range of postmodernist goals and policies while still maintaining a broad socialist agenda. The evolution of FMLN-FDR in El Salvador from a coalition of Leninist sects to a broad multilayered left movement including electoral parties, guerrilla groups, trade unions, cultural fronts and popular organizations; the labour-cum-ecological activism that Chico Mendes represented in the Amazon region before his assassination; the movement towards Socialism (MAS) in Venezuela; the Brazilian Workers Party and a host of women's groups, represent other examples of left postmodernism. Religious revival in Latin America, India and the Muslim World is a reaction against postmodernisms of both right and left. Whatever its political colour, postmodernism retains its penchant for hybridity, relativism and heterogeneity, its aesthetic hedonism, its anti-essentialism and its rejection of "Grand Narratives" (of redemption). In Latin America, rightwing politics and religious fundamentalism, imported from the US, have made major inroads in poor and working class communities from Brazil to Guatemala.

Elsewhere, the discourse of Liberation Theology aims to replace Eurocentric conceptions of both modernity and postmodernism with an indigenous historical and cultural consciousness. The discourse of "Islamization of knowledge" promotes the same goals in the Muslim world.

Postmodernism in South-East Asia has taken a form unique to itself. Here the postmodern premise that reality and its simulacrum are indistinguishable has espoused a thriving culture and economy based on fakes. What's the difference between a real Gucci watch and a fake? "Genuine imitations" are freely available. Counterfeit CDs not only look the same as the real ones but have exactly the same sound quality making it practically impossible, even for industry experts, to tell the difference. But it's not just fake watches, cassettes and CDs that are being marketed in Thailand, Malaysia, Indonesia and Singapore. Counterfeit culture produces everything from designer clothes to shoes, leather goods, antiques, even spare parts for cars and industrial processes. An astonishing 20% of the region's economy is generated by this simulacrum industry.

The End of History

We have left open and unanswered the question whether postmodernism can have, is having or will have, a history particular to itself... or is it in fact merely a **continuity** of modernism which has entered into an accelerated phase of hypermodernism?

Is postmodern history an **actuality** or a **virtuality**?

A reply to this question depends crucially on the answer to another question that we glanced over earlier.

WOULD POSTMODERNISM BE SUCH A POWERFUL IDEA IF COMMUNISM HADN'T DISINTEGRATED?

This is really asking whether postmodernism is merely a sequel to the Cold War or was it implicit as an **accomplice** of the Cold War?

If there is any one book which encapsulates and triumphantly celebrates postmodern history as an actual reality, it is **The End of History and the Last Man** (1992) by the American historian Francis Fukuyama.
In a deliberately prophetic, evangelical tone, Fukuyama proclaims a New Gospel (from the Old English, **godspel**, "good news") at the end of our millennium.

WE HAVE BECOME SO ACCUSTOMED BY NOW TO EXPECT THAT THE FUTURE WILL CONTAIN BAD NEWS WITH RESPECT TO THE HEALTH AND SECURITY OF DECENT, DEMOCRATIC POLITICAL PRACTICES THAT WE HAVE PROBLEMS RECOGNIZING GOOD NEWS WHEN IT COMES. AND YET, THE GOOD NEWS HAS COME...

And what's this "good news" that Fukuyama can precisely date as "the most remarkable evolution of the last quarter of the 20th century"?

IN ESSENCE IT'S INCREDIBLY SIMPLE... ...A CAPITALIST PARADISE AS THE END OF HISTORY!

Jacques Derrida has turned the fire-power of deconstruction on Fukuyama's "good news" which is jubilant that liberal democratic capitalism has survived the threat of Marxism. Derrida warns us: this jubilation hides the truth from itself - "Never in history has the horizon of the thing whose survival is being celebrated been as dark, threatening and threatened."

Teleology

Curiously enough, Fukuyama invokes Marx and his predecessor, the idealist philosopher, G.W.F. Hegel, to celebrate the triumph of capitalism.

BOTH HEGEL AND MARX BELIEVED THAT EVOLUTION OF HUMAN SOCIETIES WAS NOT OPEN-ENDED, BUT WOULD END WHEN MANKIND HAD ACHIEVED A FORM OF SOCIETY THAT SATISFIED ITS DEEPEST AND MOST FUNDAMENTAL LONGINGS. BOTH THINKERS THUS POSITED THE "END OF HISTORY": FOR HEGEL, THIS WAS THE LIBERAL STATE, FOR MARX IT WAS A COMMUNIST SOCIETY.

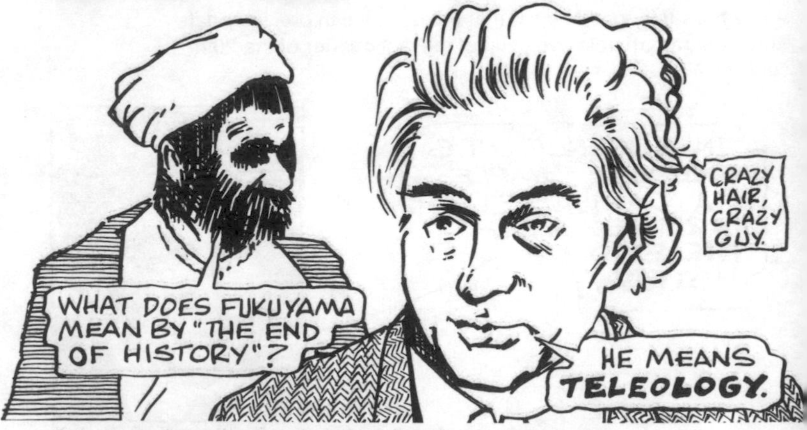
WHAT DOES FUKUYAMA MEAN BY "THE END OF HISTORY"?
CRAZY HAIR, CRAZY GUY.
HE MEANS TELEOLOGY.

Teleology (from the Greek, **telos**, "end") assumes that developments are shaped by an overall purpose or design. Therefore, the "end" of history according to Fukuyama means several things: (1) history in which Marxism played a role has **ended**, (2) because of a **purpose**, (3) which is that history has reached its end, i.e., a supreme **goal**. And what is this supreme goal?

The goal is **liberal democracy**, "the only coherent political aspiration that spans different regions and cultures around the globe." This global move towards liberal democracy goes together with a **free market** economy. Their alliance is the "good news".

Eschatology and the Last Men

If the “end of history” is teleological, the second half of Fukuyama’s title “the Last Man” involves **eschatology**. Eschatology (from the Greek **eskhatos**, “last”) is Christian theology’s doctrine of the Last Judgement - or what your present behaviour will earn in the future. Fukuyama also refers to Nietzsche’s prophecy of the “super-beings” who will replace today’s decadent “last men”. So, what Fukuyama means by “last men” are those who, in spite of enjoying all the prosperity of liberal democracy, might not welcome the end of history. They could “regress to revolution” out of sheer purposeless dissatisfaction.

FUKUYAMA CELEBRATES THE DOMINANCE OF A CHRISTIAN EUROCENTRIC HISTORY.
IT EXCLUDES ALL OTHER HISTORIES, UNLESS THEY ARE "SPIRITUALLY" CONVERTED TO LIBERAL DEMOCRACY AND THE FREE MARKET.
THAT'S WHY THE ISLAMIC WORLD, IN MY VIEW, CAN BE DISREGARDED. IT DOESN'T ENTER INTO THE GENERAL CONSENSUS WHICH IS TAKING SHAPE AROUND LIBERAL DEMOCRACY.

Virtual Reality

Derrida asks himself, why has Fukuyama's book of "good news" become such an instant best-seller in the West? Why precisely at this moment of capitalist victory is the reassurance of its survival so critically important?

Capitalism's media triumph conceals the truth that it has never been more fragile, threatened, catastrophic. Something else has surpassed both the Marxism figure-headed by a totalitarian Soviet bloc and its liberal free market opponent. This "something" is a set of hyperreality transformations in the spheres of science, technology and economics which put our traditional notions of "democracy" in grave doubt.

The crux of postmodernity is that there are two "presents". One is a "spectre" present, a Virtual Reality techno-media simulacrum that makes the other "real" present appear borderline, fugitive, elusive.

A de-materialization of the real is haunting us, making our opposition to it ineffectual. A typical example of this is the Western world's media representation of disaster - the relief of mass famine in Ethiopia is stage-managed as a rock concert charity event. Tragedy is a momentary virtuality not "really" permissible in postmodernity.

Against an insolent postmodern Gospel that dares to proclaim liberal democracy as the realized "end" of human history, Derrida protests...
.....never have violence, inequality, exclusion, famine, and thus economic oppression affected as many human beings in the history of the Earth and of humanity... no degree of progress allows one to ignore that never before, in absolute figures, have so many men, women and children been subjugated, starved or exterminated on the Earth.

A Post-Marxist Repentance

Derrida is the bad conscience at Marx's funeral. His disapproval of Fukuyama's brand of neo-rightwing po mo, passing off as "liberal", means that he has to back-pedal and admit the "Marxist" element in deconstruction.

Derrida represents a pre- "post"-modern generation, those who underwent another sort of "end of history" in the late 1950s, the oppositionists trapped between two equally unacceptable Cold War orthodoxies: pro-American capitalism and Soviet bloc Stalinist Marxism.This ideological stalemate, Derrida says, was the origin of deconstruction.

Endgame...

Can we imagine how postmodernism might **end**? End in what? It doesn't even have a specifiable **beginning**, as we've seen, but is a continued **enmeshment in modernity**. Certain strands look new, but aren't.

1. The disappearance of a player, "Communism", from the scene - foreseen in the late 50s but not really believable.

2. Cyberspace - the sum total of information technology and megamedia - is the product of **hyper**-modern developments.

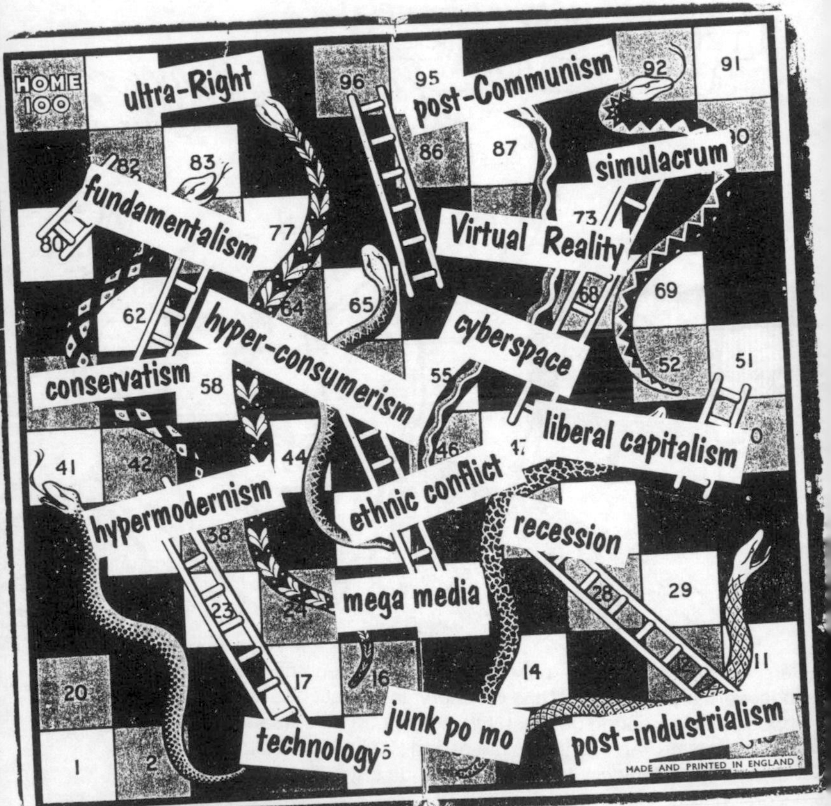

Return of the "Grand Narrative" Philosophers?

Shortly before his death (1984), Foucault called for a re-thinking of the Enlightenment. The Grand Narrative philosophers who seemed off the agenda are suddenly back on again.....

Another "spectre" is waiting to make its reappearance. **Romanticism.** Perhaps this spectre will bring the homeopathic remedy we're looking for.

The only cure for postmodernism is the incurable illness of romanticism.

Bug-eyed into the 21st Century

We've turned a century older since this book was first published in 1995. "Y2K", in the jargon of global media corporation CNN, heralded some inevitable catastrophe. Many were in "bug-eyed" fear of a worldwide information crash as computers clocked in 2000. A virus of anxiety plagued us. Our secret wish for the real languished on an anorexic diet of instant news coverage. Disasters had become chronically ephemeral. Jean Baudrillard could be relied on for wry scepticism. Already, in 1992, he had pronounced "the year 2000 a non-event".

PROPHESYING CATASTROPHE IS INCREDIBLY BANAL. THE MORE ORIGINAL MOVE IS TO ASSUME THAT IT HAS ALREADY OCCURRED.
Happy New Year
HISTORY IS WIPED FROM OUR MEMORY EVERY DAY BY THE MEDIA.

Did you wish for "9/11" too?

An act of terrorism unprecedented in history earned the epitaph of two anonymous numbers, "9/11". Baudrillard dared to test our "shock of the real" experienced on that day. For him, September 11th was the image taking cruel revenge on a world become virtual simulacrum. Al-Qaeda's unforgivable crime was to hijack the media "at last for a real event" - real because it had undeniably genuine symbolic significance. But that significance must be understood as a reality sourced in our own inadmissible guilt which can be formulated as...

September 11th does not represent Third World envy of our wealth and privileged freedoms. It represents us - Westerners who wished to see America punished for the prosperity it guarantees us.

The Fourth World War

Our ambivalence towards America assisted in September 11th. Without that added dimension of significance, on which the terrorists relied, 9/11 is simply a crime by fanatics in need of reprisal. Baudrillard is not denying the immorality of Al-Qaeda. But he wants us to focus on the **unease of conscience** involved in globalization. We have undergone three World Wars so far. The Third ended with the Cold War defeat of Communism in 1989. Each of these wars went further in the direction of a single hegemonic world order - and increasingly unpredictable resistance to it.

War on Terrorism...as seen on TV

This global war appears elusive, says Baudrillard, because terrorism proliferates like some fractal virus generated by the global system's own auto-immune defences. In these circumstances, the very idea of war itself has to be preserved, no matter how virtually unreal it now is. Hence why America must visibly enact "war on terrorism" in high-profile displays of colossal fire-power, first in Afghanistan and then Iraq. It must regain incontestable "Star Wars" dominance over the world.

The Clone in the Scrap-yard

The media-conscripted war in Iraq has taken place. Never before has a war excited such concern for "democratic legality". In disregard of worldwide protests and UN resistance to it, America went it alone, except for British support. Hollywood's paranoid nightmare scenarios of "alien invasions" had been realized by terrorist "sleepers" on September 11th. Raising the stakes on war depended on convincing other than Americans that terrorism posed a similar danger to them.

We risk chemical, biological and "dirty bomb" attacks to the extent that the Cold War left an immense scrap-yard of such useless deterrents in the former Soviet Union and other unstable countries.

Virus or Blowback?

Noam Chomsky reminds America why it is so hated. US foreign policy stands incriminated of "state terror" aid to vicious dictatorial regimes, including formerly that of Saddam Hussein in Iraq. Chomsky is a libertarian gadfly who just looks at the facts. He notes that President Carter's National Security Advisor Zbigniew Brzezinski boasted of "entrapping the Soviet Union" in a costly Afghanistan war in 1979 to hasten Communism's demise in 1989. Pentagon and CIA strategists also enlisted the "Afghani Arab" Mujahidin in this anti-Communist jihad who would form the nucleus of Al-Qaeda.

The New Bolsheviks

Baudrillard's Fourth World War idea accords with Chomsky's factual countdown to 9/11. Al-Qaeda's Islamist terrorism, created by US strategic blowback, has filled the vacuum left by the disappearance of "alternative socialism" in the Soviet Union. Does this make the Islamists the new Bolsheviks? We often hear that Islamist terrorism has no interest in the poor and dispossessed. It has another agenda. So, apart from Quranic arabesques, what do Islamists want? Women in veils? Taliban-style fundamentalist puritanism? Or something unimaginably ambitious…

The Liberal Consensus

Back in 1994, Derrida savaged Fukuyama's happy ending to history. He remarked then on Fukuyama's omission of the Islamic world as a negligible exception to the global consensus forming around America's ideal of liberal democracy. America had in fact "already realized" its pluralist free-market ideal that everyone must embrace "in the end". Derrida's indignation was prophetic; but Fukuyama did not change his eschatological tune. He now thinks that Osama bin Laden shares with Hitler the unintentional role of preparing the eventual ground for liberal democracy.

The Last Grand Narrative

Postmodern theory did not foresee that the one immovable Grand Narrative would be the United States of America. Fukuyama's vision of terminal history is really about the no-option, no-exit **endlessness of America**. The Cold War's end was supposed to liberate the world from Marxism's oppressive grand narrative. We have instead the junk capitalism of mafia pimps in East Europe and the Third World. What happened to the seedling hopes of local "micro"-narratives nursed in theory by Lyotard and other postmodernists?

The Future is Tomorrow's Past

And this is the final postmodern irony - to end up captives of an empire of perpetual postmodern hybridity. America's greatest invention is the "sell-by-date" history. When the Pentagon says "Saddam Hussein is history", it means he's **no history at all**, just obsolete. History simply isn't. Worries that we've become McDonaldized, Coke-crazed, Starbuck junkies are superficial. What matters is the global addiction to prosperity on which America's dominance relies.

The Art of Terrorism

Andy Warhol appeared to have a premonition of 9/11 in his 1963 silkscreen paintings of suicides jumping from buildings. Is he our Pop Art Nostradamus? Karlheinz Stockhausen is a German "late modernist" composer. His works are notoriously mega-Wagnerian in ambition. For instance, a string quartet premièred in 1995 requires a helicopter for each player. They fly to patterns laid out in the score and broadcast back to the ground audience. Stockhausen offensively hailed September 11th as a sublime performance…

What is Stockhausen naively confessing? That modernism has failed in its quest for the **inimitable**?

What is Postmodern Now?

Modernism is dated “post” at the dynamiting of the Pruitt-Igoe complex on 15 July 1972. How do we place the September 11th demolition of Manhattan’s World Trade Center? Consider the overlapping ironies. Minuro Yamasaki, the American-Japanese architect of the 1973 Twin Towers, was favoured by the Saudi Arabian royal family. He designed three Saudi airports. Osama bin Laden, Al-Qaeda’s mastermind, worked as a business manager in his father’s vast Saudi Arabian construction company involved in Yamasaki’s contracts. Mohammed Atta, leader of the September 11th kamikaze, was a German-trained graduate in architecture and urban planning.

Cold Comfort in Science

Fukuyama warned that history's "last men" might "regress to revolution", not from need but from dissatisfaction with prosperity. Islamic culture finds itself implicated in terrorist regression. It is not alone in facing the urgent question today. Is any culture able to resist global homogenization? Resistance assumes that culture is consciously autonomous. But is it? Survival depends on what we believe, what we do and how we see others. What if these tactics of culture are pre-coded conditions of behaviour? This is the view of neo-Darwinist evolutionary psychology. Cultures are themselves products of Darwinian natural selection, just like our genes, and generated **unconsciously** like everything else in the universe.

The End of Culture

So, if culture is meme-structured and genetically patterned; if we are trapped in our symbols, customs, religions, languages and so forth - then we are in fact blinded and handicapped by our cultures. What chance do we have of resisting our own limits? Unless, of course, a tendency to a single universally homogenous culture is also pre-programmed. Differences of culture are doomed to levelling.

IN YOUR "MEME" SCRIPT, CONSCIOUS MINDS DO NOT COUNT AT ALL...
NOT QUITE. WE ARE GIFTED WITH UNDERSTANDING THE "BLIND PROCESS" THAT GAVE US ALL EXISTENCE.

Dawkins has to admit human imagination - science would be impossible without it - but we are all still embedded in the Darwinian "algorithm of natural selection".

Beyond our Conscious Perception

String Theory is the novelty in sub-particle physics. It only makes sense in a 10-dimensional world, imperceptible to us, because the extra dimensions are wrapped invisibly small. String Theory might just be wacky "post"-physics but it conforms to the modernist scientific spirit of reducing everything - including our consciousness - to smallest bits in its quest for the Grand Unified Theory of Everything. Reality eludes us more with each step in diminution. We have forgotten the existentialist dictum of **Jean-Paul Sartre** (1905-80)…

"What we call freedom is the irreducibility of the cultural order to the natural order."

Neither God, the Cosmos nor Consciousness

V.I. Lenin (1870-1924), the original Bolshevik conspirator, had another dictum: "The worse, the better." He meant the worst conditions are the best for revolution. But that too has been reduced away by the "Grand Unified Theory" of globalized capitalism. Nothing, either postmodern relativist or regressively fundamentalist, can apparently resist that finality in the 21st century. Relativism and fundamentalism might indeed be the complicit twins of postmodernity.

The remedy advised in 1995 now looks even more perilous. **The only cure for postmodernism is the incurable illness of romanticism.**

Further Reading

You can download everything on postmodernism, except what it means. Information is useless without the guiding shape of ideas. These books will be useful.

The essential book remains J.-F. Lyotard's **The Postmodern Condition: a Report on Knowledge** (1979), Manchester University Press, 1992.

Original debates are outlined in the anthology edited by Hal Foster, **Postmodern Culture**, Pluto Press, London, 1985.

Another general approach is supplied by Thomas Docherty, **Postmodernism: a Reader**, Harvester Wheatsheaf, London, 1993.

Steve Connor's **Postmodernist Culture**, Basil Blackwell, Oxford, 1991, offers a clear introduction.

Fredric Jameson, **Postmodernism or the Logic of Late Capitalism**, Verso, London, 1991, kick-started the 'post'-Marxist assessment. It should be read with the brilliant but difficult Jacques Derrida, **Specters of Marx**, Routledge, London, 1994.

Charles Jencks, **What is Postmodernism?**, Academy Editions, London, 1986, illustrated the early heroic case for postmodern art and architecture.

I recommend the anti-postmodern case argued by Christopher Norris in **The Truth About Postmodernism**, Blackwell, Oxford, 1993, although it is hard reading for the uninitiated.

Icon Books publishes accessible essay-length titles in its 'Postmodern Encounters' series. I can recommend as helpful Stuart Sim's **Derrida and the End of History**, 1999, and Christopher Horrocks' **Baudrillard and the Millennium**, 1999, in this series. A compendium of these essays on postmodern cyber-communications and other related topics is entitled **The End of Everything**, foreword by Will Self, Icon Books, Cambridge, 2003.

The effects on feminism of postmodern trends and theories are usefully mapped by Sophia Phoca and Rebecca Wright's **Introducing Postfeminism**, Icon Books, Cambridge, 1999.

For an Islamic account of the Salman Rushdie affair, consult **Distorted Imagination** by Ziauddin Sardar and Merryl Wyn Davies, Grey Seal Books, London, 1990. These same authors have published the best-seller, **Why Do People Hate America?**, Icon Books, Cambridge, 2002, an excellent study of September 11th. Or you can try a collection of interviews with Noam Chomsky, **9-11**, Seven Stories Press, New York, 2001. Also suggested is Malise Ruthven's **A Fury for God: the Islamist Attack on America**, Granta Books, London, 2002.

Acknowledgements

The author is indebted to Zia Sardar and Patrick Curry for their advice and prompt written contributions. His thanks also to Charles Jencks for permission to reprint his **TLS** letter and David Lomas for his helpful study on Picasso, '**Les Demoiselles d'Avignon** and Physical Anthropology', in **Art History**, volume 16, no. 3, Sept. 1993.

The illustrator thanks his typesetters Sarah Garratt and Paul Taylor, his picture researchers Helen James, Chris Rodrigues, Isabelle Rodrigues, Glenn Ward and Duncan Heath, and photographer Robin Christian.

Biographies

Richard Appignanesi is the originating editor of Icon Books' **Introducing** series. He is the author of **Introducing Existentialism**, Icon Books, Cambridge, 2001, and the novel **Yukio Mishima's Report to the Emperor**, Sinclair-Stevenson, London, 2002.

Chris Garratt is the well-known **Biff** cartoonist in **The Guardian** newspaper, and is one of Icon's champion illustrators.

Ziauddin Sardar is a polymath and prolific writer whose prodigious output for Icon alone is worth visiting on **www.iconbooks.co.uk**

Patrick Curry, writer and historian, is the author of **Introducing Machiavelli**, Icon Books, Cambridge, 2000.

Index